#516

Coaching For Improved Work Performance

Coaching For Improved Work Performance

Ferdinand F. Fournies

F. Fournies & Associates, Inc.
Management Consultants
Bridgewater, N.J.

VNR VAN NOSTRAND REINHOLD COMPANY
New York

Library of Congress Catalog Card Number: 77-25199
ISBN: 0-442-24460-5

Manufactured in the United States of America

Published by Van Nostrand Reinhold Company Inc.
115 Fifth Avenue
New York, New York 10003

Van Nostrand Reinhold Company Limited
Molly Millars Lane
Wokingham, Berkshire RG11 2PY, England

Van Nostrand Reinhold
480 La Trobe Street
Melbourne, Victoria 3000, Australia

Macmillan of Canada
Division of Canada Publishing Corporation
164 Commander Boulevard
Agincourt, Ontario MIS 3C7, Canada

15 14 13

Library of Congress Cataloging in Publication Data

Fournies, Ferdinand F
    Coaching for improved work performance.

    Includes index.
    1. Supervision of employees.   2.   Personnel manage-
ment.   I.   Title.
HF5549.F65   658.3   77-25199
ISBN 0-442-24460-5

To
BETTY

Introduction

Much of the information in this book has been presented to thousands of managers in my seminar called "Coaching for Improved Performance." The reason for the overwhelming popularity of this seminar is perhaps explained in one manager's comments, "I have been going to management seminars for years, and this is the first time anyone has ever told me how to do specific things to solve my people management problems." This book is the result of managers' requests for more information about *Coaching*.

It is *not* the objective of the book to help managers make people happier in their work, to make managers more popular, or to raise humanity to some higher level of existence in life, although these things may occur as tangential benefits from the effective use of the coaching process. The coaching process is a technique that helps managers more successfully bring about performance achievements in business that relate directly to the survival of that business. The single purpose of this book is to help managers do better what they get paid to do, to improve their subordinates' performances, quantitatively and qualitatively, through specific, face-to-face techniques called coaching. If you apply these techniques, you will be able to modify problems with subordinates, and you will be able to change their behavior.

The book is intended to perform two separate functions. The first deals with certain specific beliefs managers have about their subordinate workers, about themselves as bosses, and about the seemingly undefinable process called management. Some managers fail in their efforts to solve people-performance problems by not doing the right things and, frequently, by doing the wrong things, because of what they wrongly believe about their subordinates, themselves, and the work relationship. For example, the president of a food processing company makes the following statement and practices it, "If I have a man who is not doing a good job, I give him a big raise. If he doesn't rise to it and get better, I fire him." Therefore, the first function of this book is to change your thinking about certain key beliefs relative to workers, bosses, and management.

The second function of this book deals with the techniques you can use as a manager to solve people-performance problems. As experience shows, even those managers who believe the right things don't know what to do about them. One of the primary reasons for this is that the management literature offers abundant theories of good management but lacks enough specific techniques. Therefore, this book will present specific techniques, to be used when you are faced with specific problems, and will tell you how to use them.

It is a natural tendency for most readers, especially experienced managers, to read only those sections of a book that appear exciting from the contents. It may seem logical to go directly to the conclusions without wasting time on the fancy explanations, and it does save time, but frequently it is as unrewarding as hearing only the punch line of a good joke.

I suggest you read the whole book from beginning to end; otherwise it will not perform its function for you. Quite simply, if you do not believe the things in the beginning, you will not do the things at the end, because they will not make sense to you. Conversely, merely believing the right things is not enough; you must do the right things to be successful.

FERDINAND F. FOURNIES

Contents

1
Why Managers
Fail As Coaches

In the first national study I conducted to analyze the effectiveness of management-performance-appraisal programs, most companies stated that the most important part of their appraisal program was the appraisal interview—the face-to-face meeting between the manager and the subordinate. When asked what was the weakest part of their appraisal program, most companies answered, *the face-to-face meeting between the manager and the subordinate.* Companies frankly admitted that if the appraisal interview was conducted at all it was usually quite ineffective. Individual managers admitted they felt ineffective in handling these face-to-face meetings, especially if the purpose was to solve performance problems. In many instances the situation seemed to be worse after the discussion than before it. The strange fact was that most of the companies recognizing managers' failure in the face-to-face process did not provide training in *how to do it.*

It was puzzling that in spite of the abundance of training programs managers have been exposed to, the majority of them were still failing to perform such a vital function of their job, the face-to-face process.

After reviewing the kinds of training managers have been exposed to, it became obvious why they were having no more success managing people today than fifty years ago. The reason is that most training requires managers to become psychologists first, before they become successful managers. These programs were telling managers *what they should do,* but not *how to do it.*

I had the chance to observe a good illustration of this problem several years ago while training one company's sales managers. Prior to the beginning of my seminar, a consulting psychologist, who had been providing salesman-selection testing for that company for over twenty years, was finishing his presentation. He was recommending how the sales managers could be more successful in their salesman-hiring practices. At the end of his presentation he said, "Gentlemen, the last and most important advice I want to leave with you is this. Before you hire a sales applicant, make sure he is motivated to sell or he will fail. I cannot emphasize this to you too strongly."

Immediately a sales manager in the back of the room raised his hand and asked, "Sir, could you please tell me what questions I should ask to find out whether or not the applicant is motivated to sell?" The speaker's response was, "I can't tell you exactly how to do that." My immediate thought was, "Mr. Consultant, if you can't tell them exactly *how* to do it, why are you telling them they *should* do it?" This problem is common in management training.

From a practical point of view, the real question is this, "If it takes a person seven or eight years of study to get a Ph.D. as a psychologist and another five to ten years of experience to be effective, how is it possible for that person to teach what he knows to someone else in two hours, two months, or, for that matter, two years?" The answer is, "It is not possible." What actually happens is that managers attend management training courses and become familiar with the theories psychologists use in their practice. They leave the training course with an even more detailed understanding of how vast their problems are, a more intense sense of urgency regarding their resolutions, and a greater willingness to try to do the right things. But they do not have the specific knowledge of *what to do.*

As a result, managers assume the role of amateur psychologist. Managers can't be blamed for this; the amateur psychological approach feels good and appears to be the only game in town, if you want to give up the Y, S, and T approach (Yelling, Screaming, and Threatening). Besides, if you believe you know your subordinate is schizoid, who is to prove you wrong?

The fact of the matter is that it is unrealistic for a manager to expect to be able to perform as a psychologist without spending time in the study and practice necessary to become one. No matter how current you may be in reading *Psychology Today* or *Reader's Digest* no one is going to send your Ph.D. to you in the mail. If you don't have a couch in your office you don't even have a running start.

I am not blaming managers for their eagerness to play the role of psychologist or their illogical belief that they *are* playing the role successfully. I place the blame squarely on the shoulders of trainers. They are trying to teach in two days what it has taken them years to learn. What they really should be doing is acting as translators. They should be translating theories and technical jargon they have taken years to learn into practical information and techniques a manager needs to know and is able to use successfully. They should be giving you information you can use without going back to college for three years.

My best advice to you is to resist the temptation and the persuasion of pseudotrainers to be an amateur psychologist. There is no such thing. Don't be seduced by the use of words and ideas you really don't know anything about. This is self-destructive behavior. It may seem like the only game in town right now, but, when you finish this book, you will know better.

CONFUSION ABOUT WHAT MANAGEMENT IS

In seminars I like to ask a simple question, which makes managers shuffle their feet: "What is management?" After some silence the usual responses are:

making a profit,
planning and achieving objectives,
getting results, and, *finally*,
getting things done through others.

When Lawrence Appley was president of the American Management Association, he made a series of films about management. The first film was directed exclusively to identifying management as *getting things done through others*. Mr. Appley said, "When you do things yourself you are a technician, when you get things done through others you are a manager." Most of us in our day-to-day management role frequently change hats. At times we close the door and do things ourselves (technician things); at other times, when we open the door and do management things, we are getting things done through others.

Too frequently many of us fail however, because we spend more time doing things ourselves than getting them done through others. Sometimes this is because we don't know any better, other times it is because the organization imposes tasks on us that are not management tasks.

In 1973, I published a national study of management performance appraisal programs[1] which analyzed the management-performance-appraisal programs in thirty-five U.S. companies. The smallest employed 100 people, and the largest employed 265,000; all were business organizations managing for profits. One of the objectives in our analysis was to identify all the items that companies measured when assessing management performance and to determine how many of these items were measured in all companies. Before you read further, make your own guess as to how many similar items of performance were measured by the thirty-five companies.

The answer was none. There was no single item of performance that all companies measured, although they were all appraising management performance. The one item that was measured by most companies was *Results* (measured by 78 percent of the companies). The next most frequent item was *Leadership* (measured by 69 percent) and *Willingness to act* (measured by 65 percent). No doubt you are similarly amazed. Why didn't all companies measure something called *delegating,* or *follow-up,* or *controlling,* or *coordinating*? These certainly are elements of performance in all management positions.

In 1975, I published another study of salesman performance appraisal programs[2] which analyzed salesman-performance-appraisal programs in seventy-five U.S. and Canadian companies. Guess how many similar items of salesman performance were measured by these companies.

Five items were measured by all companies and three other items were measured by 69 to 100 percent of the companies. Some items, such as *knowledge,* were measured as many as four times by some companies. For example, they measured separately company knowledge, product knowledge, competitive knowledge, and customer knowledge.

[1]Ferdinand F. Fournies, *Management Performance Appraised—A National Study* (Bridgewater, NJ: F. Fournies & Associates, Inc., 1973).
[2]Ferdinand F. Fournies, *Salesman Performance Appraisal—a National Study* (Bridgewater, NJ: F. Fournies & Associates, Inc., 1975).

One seemingly obvious reason for this significant difference is that management is much more dynamic and more difficult to define than selling. Unfortunately, that is not so. There are actually more differences between the different kinds of selling jobs in companies than there are differences between the different management jobs in companies. In other words, there is more similarity in the function of management in different companies than similarity in the function of selling in different companies. The job of selling varies considerably depending upon the product, the customer group, and the market. There are far fewer variables in the relationship between managers, workers, and the work, in the function of management. The obvious conclusion from this disparity in what is measured is that WE KNOW MORE ABOUT WHAT SELLING IS THAN WE DO ABOUT WHAT MANAGEMENT IS.

One of the reasons for this is that the training in management and the training in selling have taken two significantly different directions. In selling, the training objective has been to increase sales productivity, with the emphasis on teaching sales people how to do specific things to be more successful. The emphasis in management training has been primarily theoretical: increasing managers' knowledge, but not their ability to apply that knowledge. This is evidenced by the difficulties that arise when managers talk about management. It is common for managers not to recognize the difference between management practice, strategies, objectives, behavior, and characteristics.

The result is that managers are able to describe what they believe to be reasons why people are not performing correctly, but they have difficulty describing what the performance would look like if it got better. The language of management in explaining the reasons for the behavior of others involves generalizations and undefined metaphors.

For example, a vice president running a large distribution center told me in confidence that his number two man *was not cutting the mustard*. I asked him what seemed to be the problem and he replied, "The man is not pulling his own weight." When I asked what specifically he was doing wrong, the answer was "He hasn't been on the band wagon since he got the job." The conversation continued like that for another few minutes until I finally told him "I don't know what you are talking about." If that vice president had told one of his peers "My number two man is not cutting the mustard," the likely response would have been, "Do you have a replacement yet?"

If the company experts who design programs to appraise management performance do not know what management is, how can individual managers, who have spent far less time analyzing the process, know any more, or even as much, about it? Ask yourself this question, "If I, as a manager, do not know what I do as a manager, how then can I measure it in others, much less teach them how to do it?" The answer of course is, "You can't."

One of the problems goes back to the way people get to be managers. What happens is that you are called in and asked to kneel down. The big boss touches your shoulder with Excalibur and says the magic words: "I now pronounce you manager; go thither and yon and do it." You jump to your feet and smile happily, saying, "Yes, I will go thither and yon and do it." But let's suppose that instead of knighting you as a manager, the boss says, "I knight you Piper Cub pilot; go thither and yon and do it." Will you jump up and say, "Yes, I will"? Or will you respond with, "Are you kidding? I don't know what one is, much less what to do if I found one." The likelihood is that, even if you knew how to start one, you would probably crash if you tried to fly it.

It would be more logical for a person just knighted as a Piper Cub pilot to say, "Thank you very much but I don't know how to do it." So why doesn't anyone say that when someone knights him as a manager? How did he learn to do it? Flying an airplane is *things you do*; management is *things you do*. Why, in one instance, is a person willing to admit he doesn't know how to do the right things, but, in the other instance, he assumes he knows how to do the right things?

The problem becomes compounded when you realize that the boss who knighted you as a manager now believes you are one. It goes like this: "*You are one because I just made you one; therefore you must know how to do it*." This assumption sounds just as ridiculous for a manager as it would for a pilot. Unfortunately, we spend a great deal of time in business telling newly appointed managers about the things that should be done, but not the way to do them. Subsequently, when a manager fails, the primary reason for failure is assumed to be an unchangeable, inherent limitation in the individual, rather than an inability to do something because he or she DOES NOT KNOW HOW TO DO IT.

The first question I ask when someone's failure is pointed out to me is, "Who taught him how to do it?" The usual answer is, "No one."

In summary, although it seems logical to believe you know how to manage because you are a manager, that kind of thinking is out of touch with reality. If you don't find out what to do, all you have to go on is your good intentions, and good intentions do not justify ineffectual performance. *Management is things you do* to get things done through others. The things you do might be categorized under the headings of planning, organizing, directing, coordinating, and controlling, with a volume of specifics under each heading. If you can't describe to somebody else *the things you do* as a manager, then either you don't know what you are doing or what you are doing is magic, and there just isn't any magic in business. If you don't know what you are doing, you can't teach your subordinates how to do it, much less measure whether or not they are doing it correctly. The only choice left to you is to find out what it is you do, or should do, as a manager. I plan to help you do that.

WHAT DO MANAGERS GET PAID FOR?

Another obstacle to face-to-face management is what managers believe about *what managers get paid for*. When I ask managers what they get paid for, the customary responses are:

for managing,

for directing others,

for reponsibility,

for results.

I am always surprised at the variety of responses from managers who are getting paid to be managers. Many managers say, "The answer depends upon the level of the individual manager in the organization and the type of people he or she is managing." I have had Ph.D. managers and M.D. managers in certain research organizations tell me they thought they were paid *to be there.* One M.D. manager, responsible for the performance of eight subordinates who are also M.D.'s, told me that what he did really wasn't management: "It is sort of like a club." You might have assumed that if a person is getting paid for doing something, that person would know what it is he is being paid for.

Picture me at a bowling alley. I'm wearing $40 bowling shoes, $60 bowling slacks, and a $90 bowling shirt, hand-embroidered in Japan. On the back of the shirt is a bowling ball with lightning shooting out of it, pins flying in the air, and, in gold lettering, *Ferd the Champ*. I've got the most expensive bowling ball you can buy, and my bowling bag is made of unborn calfskin. My bowling score is 27. Is it likely, if you know all this, that you will come up to me, pat me on the shoulder, and say, "Ferd, you are a great bowler"? The answer is obviously *no*.

Of course, I protest, and claim that I am being misjudged. I can explain the origins of bowling and how it has changed; I can talk fluently about the different styles and nuances of bowling techniques, and I call your attention to the beauty and symmetry of my style, including my body English at the foul line. "I really am a good bowler," I say. You will probably tell me that I look good, but the final measurement of me as a bowler is my score, how many pins I knock down. It's the results that count.

Now I ask you to picture me as a manager on the job. I wear $300 suits, $40 shirts, and $20 ties. I stand tall, and carry myself with a distinguished bearing; I speak well and with authority; I am conversant with all the psychological theories of management and discourse fluently about the nuances of these theories. However, most of my subordinates are failing in their performance. Is it likely you or anyone else in the organization, knowing all these facts, will pat me on the shoulder and say, "Ferd, you are a great manager"? Once again, the answer is obviously *no*.

You are quite correct, of course, because what you are telling me is that, just as in bowling, managers get paid for results, the achievements or nonachievements of the people they manage. The success or failure of my subordinates represents my score. What this means to you as a manager is that the rewards and punishments you get as a manager— your raises, promotions, demotions, and nonpromotions—are based on the measurement of your success. These measurements of your success are not the things you do; they are the things your people do, the result. When your people are successful, you will be recognized as a successful manager. When your people are failing, you will be recognized as a nonsuccessful manager no matter what *you* are doing. The *results* of what your people do is your score.

In other words, if your subordinates are failing, it would not be appropriate for you to look in the mirror and recognize yourself as an outstanding manager or to commend yourself on the wonderful things you are doing as a manager. A pitfall of not knowing what managers get paid for leads you to believe that it is your prerogative whether or not you spend your time and effort to help a subordinate succeed. It is easy to visualize yourself as an important deity who dispenses discipline, favors, and wisdom to those members of the common mass you *wish* to favor. Unfortunately, it is not your choice; it is your job. It is self-destructive not to help them.

Picture yourself at the bowling alley faced with a split you don't like. You choose not to bowl your next ball; you tell the scorekeeper, "I choose not to try to make that split, just score me down for it." Sounds dumb, doesn't it? Of course it would be dumb if you did that. But I don't believe you would do that, because you know it would hurt your score if you did; you know it would be self-destructive behavior. As a manager, any time you choose not to help your subordinates succeed you are involved in self-destructive behavior. You are choosing to lower your score.

Your ability as a manager is measured by what your subordinates do, not by what you do. Therefore, the facts of life dictate that, as a manager, YOU DON'T GET PAID FOR WHAT YOU DO, YOU GET PAID FOR WHAT YOUR SUBORDINATES DO.

WHO NEEDS WHOM?

Another reason managers tend to fail in the face-to-face process is because they have disproportionate views of relevant values regarding themselves, their subordinates, and the company. This is not only a reason for taking the wrong action to solve subordinates' problems, but also one that prohibits managers from taking the right action, which conflicts with that belief. As a case in point, let's assume you are a manager with ten people answering directly to you. Let's also assume that today you took the day off for the express purpose of reading this book, but all of the ten people answering to you went to work. Keeping that in mind, answer this question:

If the total work load that is expected to be accomplished by you and your unit on any day represents 100 percent, what percentage would you estimate will be accomplished today with you at home and all of your subordinates on the job?

When I ask managers this question, their answers range between 70 percent to 110 percent. Now let's suppose that tomorrow you go to work, but all ten people who answer to you stay home. Now answer the question:

Of the total work load expected to be accomplished by you and your work unit, what percentage will be done tomorrow?

If your answer is above 10 percent, you are kidding yourself. The moral of the story is YOU NEED THEM MORE THAN THEY NEED YOU. It doesn't mean you are not needed. It doesn't mean you are not important. It just means that you need them more than they need you.

You might say this is an unfair example because it is only for one day. So let's do it for a longer period. You stay out for six months and they go to work every day. We will plot daily productivity and average it when the six months are up. Then you go in and they stay out for six months. We also average your productivity for the period. There will still be large differences between the averages.

This is quite contrary to what managers believe when they first become knighted as managers, and many of them never change. What happened when you were knighted? Did you rise from your knee with a smile, nodding agreement? Did you stride back to your area of responsibility with assurance? Perhaps the partitions of your office were extended all the way to the ceiling. You might have received a reserved parking space. Did you look around at the lowly masses with confidence because you knew you were true royalty? After all, you used to be one of them and you were chosen as a manager, not one of them. So why shouldn't you believe you are better than they are?

Almost immediately you realized there were numerous things those subordinates could not do unless you affixed your signature or otherwise approved. Additionally, you found they frequently came to you and asked for assistance, information, and assurances about the numerous things they had to do. You used to do what they do, and if you were promoted, it must have been because you did it better than they did. Therefore, one of your contributions now is to tell them to stop doing whatever they are doing the way they are doing it and to start doing it your way, because your way is obviously the best way. Slowly you come to the realization that you are the most important person in the group; the others depend on you for your power and the gems of wisdom that drop from your lips. The greater the frequency of their coming to you for information and approval, the more convinced you are that you are the hub of the universe. You truly wonder how they can get along without you. After all if you weren't there to sign and initial all those approvals and give the yeses and noes, and let the gems of wisdom drop from your lips, all those subordinates of yours would be lost like poor little lambs gone astray. Even on those days when you feel ill you drag yourself to work because you know they can't get along without you.

Another thing that happens to you when they knight you as a manager is that you are corrupted by power. When you are knighted, an invisible sign appears in the center of your forehead and flashes on and off: BOSS . . . BOSS . . . BOSS. You can't see it, but everyone who works for you can. You see lines of people standing around waiting to talk to you. The people who talk to you do it with deference. You notice that your subordinates seem to be concerned about the way they talk to you, but you see no reason why you should be concerned about the way you talk to them. You become aware that when you ask people to do things they do them. After all, they are only there to do your bidding. Quite happily, most of them do so, except the incompetent ones. Because people around you do what you tell them, you become even more impressed with your own importance. But what has happened is that you have become deluded into believing that you are the most important member of that group. Because you believe they need you more than you need them, you treat them accordingly. You get involved in self-destructive behavior. You get lazy and you stop managing; you just keep score.

The sad but true fact is that YOU NEED THEM MORE THAN THEY NEED YOU. You can't get the job done without them.

2
So What Does
All This Mean?

To be successful as a people manager, you must recognize three very important basic facts about your role as a manager:

Fact No. 1—Management is getting things done through others.
Fact No. 2—You need your subordinates more than they need you.
Fact No. 3—You get paid for what your subordinates do, not for what you do.

If you accept these three basics, you will come to some very important conclusions about the most appropriate behavior necessary for you to become a successful manager. For example, if management is getting things done through others, and you need them more than they need you, and you get rewarded and punished for what they do, not for what you do, the obvious conclusion is that the only reason for you to be there as a manager is TO DO EVERYTHING IN YOUR POWER TO HELP THEM BE AS SUCCESSFUL AS POSSIBLE. YOU SUCCEED ONLY WHEN THEY SUCCEED.

If you accept the fact that judgments about your performance are made not on what you do, but on what your people do, a logical conclusion is that the only way for you to get a higher score is to have your people become more successful. This also means that a higher score can be achieved only if you accept full responsibility for the success or failure of your subordinates. It also means that the more successful you wish to be in the business world, the harder you must work to do everything possible to help your subordinates achieve, rather than fail.

If you truly believe your primary purpose as a manager is *to do everything possible to help your subordinates succeed*, you are acknowledging that each time a subordinate fails, IT IS ONE OF YOUR FAILURES. If you accept full responsibility for the success or failure of your subordinates, that means the last thing you do before you fire somebody is to look in a mirror and say to yourself, "You failed," and then go out and say to the subordinate, "You're fired." This is the complete opposite of customary managerial behavior, which is to look at the subordinate and say, "You failed; you're fired."

Obviously, there are times when a subordinate's poor performance is caused by inherent limitations in that individual, and is, therefore, beyond your control. But this rarely occurs as a real cause for failure. This is in contrast to the tendency of managers to attribute most instances of nonperformance to inherent and unchangeable inabilities of the subordinate. When a manager does the latter he is inadvertently catching himself in a cul-de-sac of nonmanagement. Quite simply, once you believe (or conclude) that a subordinate's nonperformance is occurring because of unchangeable limitations in him, you have closed the door to the pursuit of other alternatives to solving that problem. You have just put yourself out of the management of that subordinate; now you can just stand around and watch what happens.

Occasionally managers will respond by saying, "It's not reasonable to expect me to accept responsibility for my subordinates' success or failure when I take over a department with people I had no hand in hiring." Since the manager did not have a hand in acquiring the resources of that department, it appears appropriate for him to point out that the nonperformance was caused by inappropriate resources. It is also assumed that the manager has the privilege (or duty) to replace those resources before he can accept responsibility for making it run right. Because of this assumption the first step of many new managers is *to clean out the dead wood*. This *house cleaning* is a common act with lower level managers, and is most common with sales managers.

I ask these same managers what they would do about this right or privilege or duty if someone said to them, "I now pronounce you Vice President and General Manager of our Denver plant," and when they arrived in Denver they found the plant to be fifty years old, the machinery, twenty-five years old, and all the workers with twenty

years' experience. Would they still feel it their right, privilege, and duty
to shut down the business, to build a new plant, buy new machinery,
and hire new employees? The answer of course is *no*. The fact is that
this so-called privilege or duty, exercised by lower level managers to
clean house, is logical to them because they don't know what management things to do to solve their management problems. Far from being a right or a privilege or a duty, it is SELF-DESTRUCTIVE
BEHAVIOR. I am not blaming managers for their self-destructive
behavior; they don't know what else to do. The purpose of this book is
to provide managers with more alternatives to solving those problems.

DOING WHAT COMES NATURALLY IS SELF-DESTRUCTIVE

Another trap for the new manager is the *I'm only human* approach.
Let's pretend the knighting ceremonies have just concluded for you.
With the sounds of *go thither and yon and do it* still ringing in your
ears, you return to your department to do that thing called management. Since you don't know how to do it, the obvious thing for you to
do is *to do what comes naturally*. You are a new manager and you
don't yet have all the answers to managing people, so the best way to
approach the problem is to be honest and straightforward and sincere
in what you do. After all, if you are sincere and try to do the right thing,
even though it doesn't come out right, nobody can blame you for that
(even those who are hurt by what you do). As a result you blithely go
about making honest, straightforward, and heartfelt decisions with the
assurance that, even though you may be doing the wrong thing to your
subordinates, they will understand because *after all, you are sincere
and have emotions just like anyone else.*

For example, picture yourself arriving at work in the morning and
saying good morning to each of your ten employees. You greet each
employee, "Good morning, Mr. A. Isn't it a beautiful day? Good
morning, Ms. B. Isn't it a beautiful day? Good morning, Mr. C. Isn't it
a beautiful day?" By the time you get to employee number ten it is only
natural that you begin to feel like a broken record. As a matter of fact,
by the time you get to employee number five, the broken-record
syndrome may have already set in, so you wave to employees five
through ten and take care of the *good morning chore* in one swoop

with a "Hi, folks." After all you are only human, and who wants to feel like a broken record? It feels ridiculous.

As another example, let's assume you hold a brief conversation individually with each of your ten employees. You say fifteen to twenty words to each of them. When you get to employee number ten, I ask you, "What did you say to employee number one?" Your response might be, "What do you think I am, a tape recorder? How do you expect me to remember everything I say?"

It's not fair is it? You are not a computer. You are only human. It is not reasonable to expect you to remember the specifics of ten conversations. Besides, the repetition in your world bores you. But what you don't realize is that when you hold a conversation with one of your subordinates, although that subordinate may be only one out of ten subordinates to you, you are only *one out of one* to each of your subordinates. You are the only boss that subordinate has. If you talk to that subordinate once today he has all day long to think about the things you said in that single conversation. He or she is free to reconstruct the sentences, using synonym and antonym comparisons, and to worry about which words you smiled before or after, and what it all meant. Although you have ten employees in your work life, each of those ten employees has only one boss.

Picture yourself at the eighty-seventh performance of a famous Broadway show. Before the curtain rises, a member of the cast steps through the curtain and says, "Ladies and gentlemen, we have performed this show eighty-six times, and we are getting a little bored with the words and music. So today we are going to do something a little different. We are going to do some different dances, tell a few jokes we like, and change the plot around to do something more interesting." Or, suppose he says, "Ladies and gentlemen, this will be our third show today. The first show we did this morning was probably the best show we have ever done. The second show was not the best, but it was a good solid show. This one is going to be a bomb because we are pooped. Go talk to the folks who saw the first two shows; they loved it."

It sounds ridiculous, doesn't it? Well, it is just as ridiculous if you believe "just being human" is an excuse to cut short your performance with any of your subordinate employees. The day you are knighted as the boss is the day you cease to have the privilege of doing what comes naturally. There is an element of show business in management. You don't have a choice as to whether it is there or not. You can choose only to recognize it or not. You can ignore it, but you can't make it go away. The fact is that when you are in front of your subordinates, you are on stage.

As an example, let's say there are specific things you should be saying or doing with each of your employees, and it takes twenty minutes to do and say those things. By the time you finish with employee number six you are tired or bored, or feel stale, so you tell employee number seven, "Listen I'm a little bored and tired of talking about this; why don't you go talk to employee number one. I was sharp when I talked to her and she loved it."

That sounds ridiculous, too, doesn't it? You probably wouldn't do that. But you might change what you are doing so it does not bore you or it takes only ten minutes rather than twenty minutes. Unfortunately, the result is the same; you are rewriting the show for your convenience, and the audience (employee number seven) does not get to see it.

The show-business aspect becomes even more obvious when you realize that whatever you do in the presence of your employees is being interpreted by them individually. They are continuously observing your actions and making their *own* interpretations as to what those actions mean *to them*. If your subordinates don't know exactly why you are doing what you are doing, they are free and quick to make their own interpretations as to why you are doing it. For example, picture yourself getting a ticket on the way to work and stepping in slush up to your knees after you park your car. As a result you are in such a foul mood you don't say your normal *hellos*, but you growl and grump as you walk past your subordinates. In response, worker number one might think, "Gee, he's still mad at me because of that problem we had yesterday, even though I said I was sorry." Employee number two thinks, "Gee, that was a very small error we made last week, and I cleaned it up before it went too far. I guess he found out about it." Employee number three thinks, "I guess he found out last night that he's not going to get that promotion he was hoping for." Employee number four thinks, "He doesn't have to be mad at me just because I asked for a raise." Onward and onward and onward. As far as you are concerned you arrived at work in a bad mood for logical reasons. But each employee knows only that the boss didn't give him the normal greeting, and each interprets this individually.

Even if you came to work and stood in the middle of the floor with your eyes closed and arms at your sides you would have varied employee interpretations, such as:

Employee one—"He's meditating."
Employee two—"He's having a heart seizure."
Employee three—"He's just wet his pants."

Once you become a manager of people you no longer have the luxury of *doing what comes naturally*. In doing what comes naturally you are very likely involved in self-destructive behavior.

Your reactions to this might be: "You mean to say that I have to be false and can't express my normal emotions to my subordinates?" The answer to that is *no* and *yes*. Falseness is not a part of what we are talking about. We are talking about controlling your self-destructive behavior. I am just asking you to control yourself in the work situation for the same reasons you now control yourself in other situations, because not to do so is self-destructive behavior.

For example, picture yourself at the bowling alley and it's the last frame of the third game. You bowl a strike and now you have to bowl another ball. Is your reaction to that, "Holy mackerel, I have to bowl again? Gee, I'm tired and I've been bowling all night and now just because I got a strike I have to bowl again." Then you pick up your ball and drag yourself into position and, because you have been bowling all night, you just throw that last ball willy nilly. Do you do that, or do you do what every other bowler does? In spite of how many games bowled that night, you do everything possible to pep yourself up and fight all the tendencies to be tired, because this ball is just as important as all the rest, if not more important. My guess is that you would not do what comes naturally; you would do what most bowlers do, which is to do everything possible to make that last ball count. You know that if you don't pump yourself up for that extra effort, it will be self-destructive to you as a bowler. My question is: "If it seems logical to resist tendencies to be just plain human in bowling (and you don't even get paid as a bowler), why don't you resist those tendencies to be just plain human in what you earn your living at, management?"

Can you picture a salesman making the last call of the day and, because he is tired, he walks up to the customer and says, "Listen, Mr. Customer, I'm a little pooped today and I'm really not going to do a very good job of selling to you. Why don't you call up that customer I visited on my first call this morning? I was really 'up' for him and he bought a lot of products." But salesmen wouldn't do that. What they would do before the last call, as tired as they are, is to check their ties and pep themselves up in some way so their actions on this last call will be as effective as they have to be to make the sale.

I know there are managers who, when aggravated by their subordinates, slam doors, slam drawers, slam down phones, break pencils, and throw pads on the desk or across the room. These same managers, when aggravated by their bosses, do not break pencils or throw pads or slam doors or kick the boss's desk. The reason is they know it would be self-destructive behavior to do that in front of a boss. The reason they continue to do that to their subordinates is because they don't realize that it is self-destructive behavior to do so. It doesn't help managerial action; it only gets in the way.

You may feel it is quite natural to express your anger and irritation when one of your subordinates fouls up his performance. It certainly may feel natural, but it has nothing to do with management. It is actually self-destructive. It is just as self-destructive as kicking your bowling ball because you missed a split. People kick a bowling ball only once in a lifetime; they find out it's self-destructive.

Did you ever drive an automobile that burned a lot of oil? If so, did you beat the hood with a tire iron everytime you drove into the gas station to buy more oil? I really believe you didn't even though you may have wanted to. It would have been foolish and self-destructive if you had.

Did you ever have a car cut you off on the road and make you feel like ramming that car to run it off the road? But you didn't. You resisted being just plain normal because you knew it would be self-destructive to do otherwise. I have confidence in you as a human being, that you do not go through the world doing self-destructive things on purpose. That's why I am taking so much time to explain to you that many of the things you do as a manager, which you *believe to be natural and normal*, are really *self-destructive* to you as a manager.

It is not expected that you switch your emotions on and off like a light switch. But it is expected, when you realize that your reactions to your emotions are damaging your effectiveness as a manager, that you will work to improve it. For example, if you get a ticket on the way to work and step in slush up to your knees when you get out of the car, you should take a moment to calm yourself down and say to yourself, "Now look, this has nothing to do with those nice people inside; therefore, why should I go in there and emote all over them?" Then enter your office and proceed as you normally do. If you cannot *yet* control yourself to that extent, then, when you enter your office, you had better tell enough people, "I just want to let you know that I'm going to act a little weird today because I am really mad about stepping into slush up to my knees and getting a ticket on the way to work."

Let me clarify here that all emotional responses on the job are not self-destructive behavior. If you accidentally smash your hand in a file drawer, I am not recommending that you stuff the bloody stump under your arm and proceed with placid dignity. Screaming, yelling, and some foul language would be quite appropriate. Also, the spontaneous expressions of pleasure over successes (finding solutions to problems, getting the sale, eliminating errors, finishing on time or ahead of time, etc.) are not self-destructive to your management.

Not doing what you are supposed to do, however, because you are tired or bored is self-destructive behavior. Giving subordinates a rear view of wisdom teeth, or demonstrating how red in the face you can get in fits of rage over their nonperformance is self-destructive. If you must express your rage, do it in a closet; don't louse up your managerial actions by doing it all over your subordinates. DOING WHAT COMES NATURALLY IS SELF-DESTRUCTIVE BE-HAVIOR TO A MANAGER.

SELF-DEVELOPMENT AS A DESTRUCTIVE MANAGEMENT CONCEPT

Another reason managers fail in their face-to-face process with their subordinates is because they view their subordinates outside the business parameters within which they embrace all other resources they are paid to manage. When teaching managers about the process of management, I frequently ask them to list the resources they manage. The list usually looks like this:

1. machines,
2. money,
3. raw materials,
4. facilities (buildings),
5. finished product,
6. people.

The reason *people* usually ends up on the bottom of the list is because managers do not generally think of the subordinates assigned to them as a resource. Managers even ask whether it is dehumanizing to refer to people as a resource. The truth is that many managers are ineffective as people managers because they *do not* recognize the people working for them as a business resource. They do not apply the same business rules to managing people as they do to all the other resources they manage.

As an example, let's assume that I am responsible for an office building. Let's also assume there is a raging storm outside and a leak in the corner of one room. The water is coming in at the ceiling, dripping down the wall, and wetting the floor. Since I am responsible for the building, you come to me and say, "Ferd, what's going on with that leak in the corner?" My answer to you might be one of the following responses:

"Well, it's an old roof. What can you expect?"

"Well, it's a cheap roof. We didn't pay much money for it. What can you expect?"

"Well, it's a poorly designed roof. Everytime it rains we are going to have that problem."

Those are pretty ridiculous responses, aren't they? If the building were my responsibility, I would probably not respond that way. I most likely would take action to prevent the water from coming in. I would look for alternatives to solve the problem.

Let's take a look at another situation. Let's make believe I am responsible for a group of production machinery in a certain manufacturing department. You are my boss and you have just come to visit my department to see how things are going. What you hear is a very high-pitched noise similar to that of a bearing in a machine burning out due to lack of lubrication. You say: "Ferd, what's happening with that machine over there?" My possible responses to you might be:

"Well, it's an old machine, you know. You can't expect too much from an old machine."

"Well, it's a cheap machine, you know. We didn't pay too much money for it. What can you expect?"

"Well, that machine has a poorly designed lubricating system. It was that way when we got it, and the bearing is burning out."

I am sure you will again agree with me that those responses would be quite inappropriate. More likely I would be taking the necessary action to have the bearing replaced and the proper lubrication provided. As is customary in business, if our company had purchased a machine and it was later discovered that the lubricating system was not the best or didn't suit our needs, we probably would have modified it to make it work. We would seek alternatives to solve the problem.

Let's look at another example. Pretend that I am responsible for the company's cash, and I currently have $26 million in a full-service bank that is giving us 6½ percent return. Today we receive a letter from another bank that is similar in every respect except that it gives 6¾ percent return. My reaction is:

"Gee whiz, look at that. We have our money in this bank giving 6½ percent and that bank over there gives 6¾ percent. Son of a gun. Isn't that a shame?"

You are right, ridiculous again. What most likely would happen is that our $26 million would be moved to the second bank.

Now let's pretend I have a subordinate working for me who is failing, and you, my boss, say to me, "Ferd, what's wrong? Why is that human resource failing?" My possible responses to you are:

"Well, it's an old resource, you know. It has been around here for a long time. What can you expect? You can't do anything with it."

"It's a cheap resource. We don't pay much for it. What else can you expect for the money we pay?"

"It's poorly designed; you know it comes to us in a different color and speaks a different language."

How many times have you heard similar reasons given for a worker's nonperformance? Strangely enough, these responses as reasons why the human resource is not working do not sound so ridiculous. What we have here is a contradiction in the theoretical approach managers use in managing their nonhuman resources compared to their human resources.

Managers have no difficulty in accepting full responsibility for the success or failure of their nonhuman resources. As a matter of fact managers pride themselves on obtaining performance from their nonhuman resources when others have admitted defeat. In actual practice, managers diligently seek out every possible alternative to solving incidences of nonperformance of nonhuman resources. It is a source of pride to make things work in spite of obstacles. Managers stop seeking alternatives only when it is finally determined that additional efforts to make the resource work are no longer economically feasible. That is, the cost of efforts to make the resource work is greater than the value of what the resource would produce, if it did work.

Now, in sharp contrast, when managers are faced with nonperformance of their people, they try only a few alternatives and quickly surrender with, "Oops, it's beyond our control. It's the resource's fault, not ours, that performance is not what it should be." The most appropriate solution to correcting nonperformance of a human resource appears to be to replace it. One of the reasons managers do this is because they don't know what other alternatives to try, to make the human resource successful. But this is not the primary reason. The primary reason is because they believe in the concept called *self-development*, which in business means:

"We believe that all development is self-development; we, the company, provide the right environment for you, the individual, to develop yourself. We also provide the opportunities, and if you do not take advantage of these opportunities, then it is your decision to fail, not ours."

This belief predisposes managers to place the full responsibility for performance or nonperformance on the shoulders of the *human resource* itself. This is quite contrary to the manager's business approaches with all the other resources. Can you picture yourself, for example, going into your boss's office and stating that a piece of equipment you purchased twelve months ago for $30,000 was not what you really needed; that you had made the wrong purchase? If you are like most managers I know, that would be the last alternative you would select. To admit such a thing would be an embarrassment, a direct reflection on your management ability, and a source of agitation to your boss. It might even damage your career. You would most likely do everything possible to make that piece of equipment work, in spite of the fact that it was a bad purchase. But what happens when you hire a human resource for $30,000 and twelve months later that resource doesn't work out? You walk in and announce to your boss, "I don't think that Charlie is going to work out; I think we made a poor hire." The typical boss's response is, "How long will it take to get his replacement?"

Why is this announcement, which continually echoes through the halls of business, "I think we made a poor hire," made with impunity and without embarrassment? Why aren't managers just as worried about confessing their poor investment in a human resource as they are about a poor investment in a nonhuman resource?

One of the reasons is that companies have not truly calculated the cost of replacing a human resource the way they calculate the cost of replacing their nonhuman resources. When an organization is going to buy a new piece of production equipment they not only calculate the cost of the purchase and delivery of that equipment; they also calculate the cost of everybody's time, including the training time of the operator on the new equipment, until productivity reaches a specified standard. When a company replaces a human resource, however, their calculations include only the hiring fees and relocation costs. They stop calculating cost when the human resource arrives at the front door. They do not calculate the cost of everyone's time invested in that new human resource until the resource achieves performance standards. This can be anywhere from thirty days to six months. They don't even include the cost of everyone's time required in making the hiring decision.

One of the tasks I require of my M.B.A. students at the university is to choose a manager in their organization who has been recently discharged and calculate the true cost of replacing that human resource. Typical of the findings is the case of one student who was surprised to discover that the cost of replacing a $30,000 a year division controller was $30,000. When I asked him what his findings meant to him as a manager, he replied "Had I known this beforehand, I would have been willing to invest $10,000 to fix the old one rather than spend $30,000 to get a new one."

One executive, as a result of being exposed to the above ideas, calculated the following cost of replacing one of his technical, professional subordinates.

Estimated Replacement Cost for Technical Professional, Salary $25,000

1.	Severance pay @ 1 week/year of service	$ 5,000
2.	Notice to severed employee, 4 weeks (permitted to job hunt)	2,000
3.	Employment advertisements	1,500
4.	Interview expenses, 5–10 people, $300 ea., avg.	2,500
5.	Time spent by interviewers, 7–10 days @ $200/day	1,500
6.	Employee orientation	1,000
7.	Relocation	10,000
8.	Agency fee @ 25%	5,000
	Subtotal	$28,500
9.	Project orientation time (up to 6 months)	12,500
	Total	$41,000

As a result of the information he gathered, these were his comments:

My career has always been in industries where equipment was the tool for production of the product itself. I am, therefore, very familiar with the techniques and decisions relating to the risk/reward probabilities of maintenance and modification versus write-off and replacement. I have seldom considered the human resource in the same way because it seemed too impersonal, inappropriate, or not a useful standard of measurement.

The replacement costs obtained in this project were surprising. Seldom have I viewed my people as an asset that might cost me $30,000 to $50,000 to replace. Never have I considered spending even $15,000 to $20,000 to retrain or modify this asset. It is clearly evident that within the context of total replacement costs, the amount of expense justified for successful rehabilitation can be a high percentage of the annual salary and still be a profitable decision.

Here's how another manager calculated the cost of replacing a word processing typist, who uses a machine that makes a magnetic recording of what is being typed, permitting the typist to make revisions without redoing the entire document. This employee was terminated after eighteen months of employment. The costs were as follows:

Severance pay—2 weeks	$ 540.00
Recruiting advertising	525.00
Manager's interviewing time	72.74
Supervisor's interviewing time	72.74
Overtime for workload not covered by terminated employee—45 hrs.	225.00
New employee's physical	25.00
Hiring processing costs	100.00
Nonproductive wages	702.00
Total	$2,262.48

The manager concluded that if the supervisor had spent only half the above cost in trying to correct the previous employee, she could have invested 3.7 weeks of her time (at $300 per week) to fix the problem employee rather than firing her, and it would have been a profitable decision to the company.

Because managers do not realize the cost of replacing a human resource, the logical alternative to solving a people performance problem is to replace that human resource. Individual managers can't be blamed for this because normal management practice has not required the same specific cost calculation of replacing human resources they require for nonhuman replacement. The fact is, in the business world when you fire somebody, you actually suffer more than he does. Your troubles begin with the echo of your words, *you are fired.* Consider the losses in your own productive time as a manager because of the time and effort you must devote to initiating search, hiring, and training the new resource before it becomes as competent as the predecessor. If you calculate all costs, you will discover that in most instances it is more economically profitable for you and your business to improve the performance of the incumbent.

I am not recommending something new to you; I am just telling you to be consistent. You now accept full responsibility for the success or failure of your nonhuman resources, which require you to do everything possible to assist them in being successful. In fact, you demonstrate your outstanding management ability by doing everything to achieve the needed performance in spite of obstacles. The point I am trying to make is that you do not have the prerogative of approaching the management of your human resources outside of these very important business parameters. You do that only because of what you believe about that resource. If you believe the resource must develop itself, you will expect it to improve itself, and this directs you away from managing that resource. This is self-destructive behavior. To be successful as a manager, you must accept full responsibility for the success or failure of ALL YOUR RESOURCES, not just your nonhuman ones.

Along about now you are probably saying to yourself, "Wait a minute. My human resource is quite a bit different from my nonhuman resources. After all my machines don't talk back to me. Are you telling me that I should be managing my human resource the same way I manage my machines?"

Of course you are right about your human resources being different from your nonhuman resources. But if you don't stop there, you will also realize that your nonhuman resources are also different from each other. Certainly your financial resources are quite dissimilar from your equipment resources and your equipment resources are quite dissimilar from your raw materials, and so on. But I am not talking about the *way* you manage your resources, I am talking about what you believe about those resources that causes you to mismanage them.

It would be ridiculous to expect you to manage your human resources the same way you manage your nonhuman resources. How can you manage your money the same way you manage your machines or your equipment? You don't put oil on your money or your people, but you certainly need it on your machines. You don't put shingles on your machines, your money, or your people, but you certainly do put them on your facilities. The specific way in which you manage each of your resources is certainly peculiar to that resource. You are right that your people can talk back to you and your other resources cannot, but this ability to talk and to reason is an advantage for you in managing that human resource, not an obstacle. It becomes an obstacle only when you don't know what to do about it, and the purpose of this book is to help you know what to do about it.

The conclusion I want to leave you with is this. The concept of *self-development* may be appropriate for personality development, but it is self-destructive as a management concept. It is in conflict with the business parameters within which you manage all of your other resources. You, as a manager, must ACCEPT FULL RESPONSI-BILITY FOR THE SUCCESS OR FAILURE OF YOUR HUMAN RESOURCES the same as you have always accepted full responsibility for your nonhuman resources. You are the greatest influence over the success or failure of your resources. If you believe the resource must develop itself, then you will not exert that influence, which will result in your SELF-DESTRUCTIVE BEHAVIOR as a manager.

3
Motivation—The Theories You Can And Can't Use

In an effort to get you and me to the same starting point, I would like to pose the following problem for you. If you had a subordinate manager who came to you today and said, "Please tell me what I can do *tomorrow* to motivate my subordinates to increase their productivity," what would you say? Use the fly leaf or a piece of scratch paper to write down your answer before you read further.

This is a question I frequently ask managers in my seminars, and it is always surprising how long it takes to get a response. Even more surprising are the responses themselves, which usually are:

"Get to know them better."
"Talk to them."
"Get close to them."
"Let them know you're interested in them."

Occasionally someone will respond with "Enrich their jobs," which has a practical ring to it, but which is quite nonspecific. On rare occasions someone will answer:

"Set goals for them," or
"Recognize their achievement."

The scarcity and impracticality of the responses are even more surprising when you realize that managers asked this question are not neophytes. They are company presidents, vice presidents, directors, and experienced managers at all levels in all kinds of organizations, who have been exposed to the prevalent management training literature. It is also quite common for these same managers to state the reason for poor performance as *lack of motivation,* which leads us to the next logical question, *What is motivation?*

Quite often a group of twenty-five managers will spend fifteen minutes trying to define *motivation,* a word they use so freely. Invariably they settle on two definitions as follows:

1. Motivation is a thing you do to get others to do something.
2. Motivation is something that happens inside an individual that gets him to do something.

It is a wonder there is not more unanimity in defining a concept that is so heavily threaded through management training and which appears to be vitally related to success in people management. Why is it that despite all of the management training to which managers are exposed, they are able to talk about motivational theories and reasons for nonperformance, but are unable to specify practical things in their control to influence motivation? A review of some of the theories may give us a clue.

HIERARCHY OF NEEDS

One theory of motivation is that man does the things he does because of his needs; that is, man directs his own actions to satisfy his own needs. Therefore, man's needs are considered the source of all of his actions; that is, they prompt his actions. And because man has many needs at any one time, the strongest need is the need that determines man's actions at that time.

According to one behavioral scientist,[1] these needs motivate man's actions only as long as they are not satisfied; once a need is satisfied it no longer motivates. According to Maslow, these needs, to which man's actions are directed, can be categorized and compared in their relative importance as they influence man's actions. He arranges these needs in a hierarchy as indicated below. When a need at any one level is satisfied, the next level need becomes predominant.

---

[1]Abraham H. Maslow, *Motivation and Personality* (New York: Harper & Row, 1954).

As indicated in the hierarchy, the first level need is the basic human need related to the sustenance of life itself, such as food, clothing, and shelter. Once these physiological needs become satisfied, the next level need, *safety and security*, becomes predominant as a motivator. This would be equivalent to the need for self-preservation. It is not only the need to be free from the physical endangerments, but also the perception that this is so.

Once these needs, which are primarily physiological, are satisfied the next level need, *affiliation or belonging*, emerges as the dominant need. This, considered as the first sociological need, is the need to share a physical propinquity with others, but also to perceive that acceptance by the group. Once this need is satisfied, it is theorized that *esteem* becomes dominant. This is the need for the individual to be recognized by the group as being outstanding for some reason, as well as the need for self-esteem, which is based on the recognition of others.

Once esteem needs have been satisfied, the need for self actualization becomes more dominant as the motivator. Maslow says this is difficult to describe. Described in different ways by different individuals, it has to do with the individual's concepts of life and man and those things that each individual feels are needed to maximize one's potential whatever it may be. You know you have it when you feel you are doing or accomplishing in life those things you feel you should be doing.

Although it is accepted that each individual varies widely as to where he will be in the hierarchy, and that people will move to different levels of needs even though a previous level has not been fully satisfied, the assumption of this theory is that people will act in specific ways because of the dominant need that influences their behavior. For example, the need for esteem is considered to be related to prestige, power, self-confidence, and control.

When this theory is presented to managers in training seminars, the participants usually leave the seminar with the assumption that they know or will be able to know what level need is predominant with a particular individual they manage. They then assume they will be able to identify elements in the work environment that will satisfy that dominant need. Therefore, managers faced with a problem subordinate will attempt to translate the hierarchy theory of needs into specific actions, by having long conversations with subordinates *to get to know them better*. These interesting conversations cover broad areas about the subordinate's past and present life in and out of business, and past disappointments, achievements, and aspirations. Through these conversations the manager tries to identify the needs that occur within the individual, between his or her ears. The assumption is that if the boss talks to the subordinate long enough, he will know what is going on between the subordinate's ears.

There are two problems with this approach for managers, however. In the first place, to know what is going on between someone's ears just by talking to him is not an easy process even for a psychologist, and it is very difficult, if not impossible, for a nonpsychologist. In the second place, if you did know what was going on between someone's ears today, you would not know forever. If you wanted to know next month you would have to play amateur psychologist again. I am not questioning whether Maslow's theory is valid or whether or not it can be used by a psychologist. What I am questioning is whether or not you, as a manager, can use it. As a teacher, I am faced with the problem of not only telling managers what they should do but also telling them how to do it, and I can't tell managers how to put that theory to work tomorrow with any certainty of gauging success. Therefore, it is not appropriate for me as a basis for teaching you a face-to-face technique for improving subordinates' performance. Not being able to tell you *how to do it* prohibits me from telling you that *you should do it*.

THEORY X VS. THEORY Y

Perhaps you are familiar with the work of another noted behavioral scientist, Douglas McGregor, who is famous for his classification of management approaches as *Theory X vs Theory Y*.[2] According to McGregor, the structure of organizations is based on certain assumptions about human nature and human motivations. *Theory X* assumes that most people find work inherently distasteful, lack ambition, have little desire for responsibility, and prefer to be directed; they are not creative in solving organizational problems, and they want safety above all. Managers who accept *Theory X* believe that people are motivated by money, fringe benefits, and threats of punishments. *Theory X* managers believe that people work only as long as they are watched; therefore, the best management approach is to design exactly what it is that these people must do, tell them specifically what they must do, and closely control them or coerce them to make sure they do it. Managers in companies that accept *Theory X* build a top-heavy organization with many levels of managers who are planning, deciding, and policing what everyone is doing.

McGregor presented an alternate theory, *Theory Y*, which assumes that people are not naturally lazy or unreliable, and that a properly motivated worker is capable of directing his or her own efforts to accomplish organized goals. According to *Theory Y*, work is considered as natural as play if the conditions are favorable; people do have the capacity and creativity for solving organizational problems; they can be self-directed and creative at work if properly motivated and they do want to do a good job when they are doing it. Managers in organizations that accept *Theory Y* push information and responsibility downward, explaining to workers the reasons why things should be done, assuming they have an interest in doing them and a willingness to do them. Managers also spend time with workers discussing problems and asking for their ideas and suggestions as to how the job can be done better.

Unfortunately, managers who thought they were following *Theory*

---

[2]Douglas McGregor, *The Human Side of Enterprise* (New York: McGraw-Hill Book Co., 1960).

Y assumptions got themselves involved in something called *democratic management*. They met with their workers and not only explained what had to be done, but took votes on what things would be done and when. This was a misdirection in McGregor's view. Business is one of the most undemocratic organizations in our democracy. Employees do not vote on who is going to be the company president, much less who is going to be their manager. Because of the information available to any manager concerning his unit's relevancy to the entire organization, as well as that manager's upward and lateral interface relationships in the organization, there are certain decisions that can be made only by the manager. It is one thing to collect ideas and suggestions from subordinates on how a job might be done better, but it is another thing to make the decision whether or not to change the job. McGregor stressed that a manager must manage; managers must make those decisions that only the manager is able to make.

The most important conclusion that can be drawn from McGregor's *Theory X vs Theory Y* concept is not about workers, but about managers: MANAGERS DO WHAT THEY DO FOR OR TO WORKERS BECAUSE OF WHAT THEY BELIEVE ABOUT WORKERS. As mentioned earlier, managers are not as successful as they should be in the face-to-face process primarily because of their unfounded and erroneous (and self-destructive) beliefs about workers. Ask yourself if you would act differently as a manager if you *really believed* all your workers wanted to and were capable of being successful.

SATISFACTION AND DISSATISFACTION

Another noted behavioral scientist, Frederick Herzberg, initiated some revealing studies of motivational influences on the nonblue collar worker.[3] One of the most interesting realizations that comes from Herzberg's research is that the things that *dissatisfy* workers are not just the opposites of the things that *satisfy* workers. According to Herzberg's findings, things that dissatisfy workers are entirely different from those that satisfy them. The factors or relationships of the job

---

[3]Frederick Herzberg, et al. *The Motivation to Work* (New York: Wiley & Sons, 1959).

that lead to each are distinctly different. A few of the dissatisfiers and satisfiers Herzberg found in his initial research are listed below.

Dissatisfiers	*Satisfiers*
company policy administration	achievement
supervision	recognition
work conditions	work itself
salary	responsibility

The important implication of this is the realization that elimination of a dissatisfaction does not automatically provide a satisfaction. If you, as a manager, eliminate a dissatisfaction for your workers, you should not assume that you have created a *satisfaction*. You have only eliminated a dissatisfaction.

For example, Herzberg listed compensation inequities as a common source of dissatisfaction. A compensation inequity occurs when you pay two workers doing a highly similar job, highly dissimilar compensations, or when you pay two workers doing highly dissimilar jobs, highly similar compensations. What you have is unfairness, an inequity, a dissatisfaction. This kind of dissatisfaction is a common one and has nothing to do with whether your company is the highest paying or lowest paying company in town. If you do the proper thing and eliminate this inequity, using sound wage and salary administration, you will only have eliminated a dissatisfaction.

Another source of dissatisfaction in many organizations relates to the supervisory relationship caused by managers using the Y, S, and T approach (yelling, screaming, and threatening). If this is a source of dissatisfaction to workers you can take steps to eliminate it by teaching the managers to smile a lot, be friendly, and not to scream so much. If you succeed, you will merely eliminate a dissatisfaction.

The same thing relates to working conditions. You may have complaints that the work area is hot in summer and cold in winter, that the old paint is grimy, and that the seats are hard and worn. If you take steps to improve these conditions by making it warm in the winter and cool in the summer, painting the walls, and replacing the seats with softer ones, and even providing music, you certainly have taken steps to eliminate dissatisfactions. But according to Herzberg's theory, you have not created a satisfaction or motivator. When you eliminate these dissatisfiers you are merely cleaning up the environment. Herzberg refers to these activities as improving the hygiene factors. For example, picture yourself with a cavity in one of your teeth. If you take the positive action of brushing your teeth three times a day you may be successful in preventing the cavity from getting any worse, and your breath may smell nicer, but your efforts did not fill the cavity or make it go away.

Herzberg indicated that the satisfiers were motivators because they had the positive effect of increasing the individual's output. Of these satisifers he found *achievement* to be the single strongest motivator. Herzberg said that people are not motivated by failure; they are motivated by achievement. Small achievements act as motivators for someone to go on to try to achieve a *little bit more*. This *achievement* is the perception that occurs in a person's mind that he has done something for the first time or has done it better than he ever did it before. For example, picture someone who usually falls down six times every time he tries to stand up. If once he falls down only five times, he could perceive that as an achievement. That achievement then influences that person to try to stand more frequently and perhaps to try to walk. Further achievement (falling down less) acts as a motivator to pursue more achievements.

The second strongest motivator, as indicated by Herzberg, is *recognition*. This occurs when someone achieves something and someone else recognizes that accomplishment in some way. For example, suppose an individual has only fallen down five times instead of six and you run over to him and say, "Hey, you are improving your ability to stand up; you fell down less than you normally do." The words of praise for that achievement are *recognition*.

Herzberg tells us that the dissatisfiers on a job have no influence as motivators for high-level performance. The satisfiers are considered as actual influences to motivate people to higher levels of productivity. If achievement and recognition are the strongest motivational influences in the work environment, one effective way to increase productivity would be to provide more opportunities in each job for achievement to occur, which would give you, the manager, more opportunities to apply recognition. Makes sense doesn't it?

Herzberg conducted his research and published his findings almost twenty years ago. A logical question would be "What do managers do today in business because of these important findings?" For example, if achievement and recognition are the strongest motivators and lead to increased productivity, what do we managers do as a general practice to take advantage of that? The answer is *little or nothing*. In fact we behave contrary to his findings; we spend a lot of time convincing people that the good work they produce is normal—that what they *achieve* is what was expected anyhow, and that's what they get paid for. How often have you heard managers make statements similar to these:

"I wish (so and so) would grow up; every time he solves a problem he runs in here to tell me about it."

"Some people around here think they should get a medal when they do something right; I wish they would get the message that doing things right is what they get paid for."

"(So and so) would be great if he would just stop looking for a pat on the head when he does something right."

In spite of the fact that Herzberg's first work on the subject was published in 1959, it appears that managers continue to ignore the motivational influences of *achievement* and *recognition*.

A game I play with managers in my seminars is to ask them to think of the possible number of achievements that might have been accomplished by their subordinates during the last ninety days. I ask them also to include achievements that might have occurred three months ago that they just recently found out about.

Once they have written down that number I then ask them to think of a second number, the number of times they did something that might have been considered as recognition of that achievement. Then I ask them to compare their two numbers. No one has ever had two equal numbers. Rarely is anyone's first number less than four times larger than the second number. This means that for every four achievements occurring in the work place the manager is only recognizing one of them. Managers get embarrassed by this and quickly defend themselves by stating they never pass up the opportunity to recognize somebody's achievement as long as they are aware of it. They also complain they have very busy schedules and don't really have time to stroll around to find out what their subordinates are doing. They say "The theory is fine, but in the real world we have to address ourselves to the bottom line." These managers are saying they don't have time to seek out the achievements of their workers so they can recognize those achievements and thereby motivate the workers to improve, because they, the managers, are spending all their time trying to increase productivity. Sounds foolish, doesn't it?

I know an experienced manager who has had serious discussions about a subordinate's level of maturity because the subordinate persisted in waving his achievements in front of the boss. The conversation went something like this.

"You have been on the job eighteen months now and you are doing a fine job. You certainly have the kind of creativity, experience, and insight that we expected you to have when we hired you. I certainly have no complaints about the problems you have helped us to solve and the systems you have helped us to implement. However, I am seriously concerned about your maturity and self-confidence. You appear to have a great need for me to pat you on the head each time you come up with a new idea, a solution to our problems, or an innovative system change. I think it is important for you to realize that the nature of your job is to be creative, to seek out solutions, and to be innovative in implementing them. We know you are very creative and have a lot of good ideas. That's why we hired you and that's why we pay you such big dollars. You should learn to have a little more confidence in yourself and realize that for someone as gifted as you the innovative and creative processes are what you should expect as normal for yourself. We certainly expect it as normal for you. We like you and we think we have made the right choice in putting you on that job. Therefore, you should have no reasons for feeling insecure in that job. If you continue to produce as you are now producing, there certainly will be no doubts about your long-range future in this organization. I will certainly take care of you at raise time. But you should stop wasting your time and my time by expecting me to pat you on the head like a little boy each time you come up with a solution. Neither one of us has time for that. There is no need for you to worry whether we are aware of your accomplishments. Although it may not appear so at times, we are aware of what is going on and will quickly let you know if things are not as they should be."

The real message is, "Why don't you go back to your office, chain yourself to your desk, and keep pumping out those good ideas and solutions. Remember that those good ideas are really just normal productivity for you; that's exactly what is expected."

I have been with managers when they have tried to avoid recognizing achievement saying, "Uh oh, let's take a walk. Here comes so and so who wants to tell me what a wonderful job he did today." These managers think they are responding normally to an aggravation in their otherwise busy work schedules. What is actually happening, however, is that the worker is trying to communicate to his manager, "Look boss, I'm motivated because I think I just achieved something. Why don't you recognize my achievement, which will motivate me to go out and achieve more things?" The managers are responding with, "Get out of here, kid, you bother me. I don't have time to waste; I'm too busy trying to increase productivity."

Metaphorically speaking, what we have is a situation where someone (Herzberg) has told us that if you tickle people under their right ear lobe they will jump over all the tall buildings in town, but managers are running around scratching everybody's left knee cap. If managers are interested in increasing productivity, and they are aware of Herzberg's findings that recognition is the second strongest motivator to improve productivity, why aren't they spending more time seeking out achievements, which would present them with an opportunity to apply recognition. For example, why shouldn't the second number *recognizing achievements,* be 80 to 90 percent of the achievements occurring?

One of the reasons given is *not enough time.* Managers claim they don't have enough time to manage. For the last ten years I have been asking managers during seminars if they hand pay checks personally to their subordinates. Half or fewer do this. Checks are usually distributed by the manager's secretary, the payroll department, or, at worst, through the mails. Some companies have direct deposits to the worker's bank. Of those managers who do personally hand out pay checks I ask, "How many of you say 'thank you' to your subordinates when you give them their checks?" Only one out of a thousand managers do that. The rest, like one bank vice president, think I am crazy. He said, "Why should I thank them? I am giving them their pay checks, they should thank me." The assumption is that the manager is presenting a gift to the subordinate; therefore, the subordinate should express the proper gratitude. The fact of the matter is that a pay check must be given for past work done; the law requires you to do it. If you decided not to do it, there would be legal recourse to make you do it. You are not giving them a gift; you are only giving them the compensation they have earned for the work performed. And if you have not taken specific action to thank a subordinate for something (or talked to him or her) during the past work period, pay check time gives you the opportunity to express your thanks for merely coming to work every day during the period.

Another reason managers don't recognize achievement is because they are not aware of the numerous forms of recognition at their disposal. Most managers believe the only forms of recognition that have any impact on the employee are raises, bonuses, or promotions. Managers do not realize that one of the major sources of recognition is the sounds that come out of their mouth directed to their subordinates, such as:

"Thank you."

"It looks like a very good job."

"I appreciate all your effort on that."

"Thank you for working so hard to get this to me in the short time available."

"You certainly seem to be making a lot fewer errors than you used to."

"I could never do it that well."

The third and most important reason managers do not score higher recognizing achievement of subordinates is because managers have a warped sense of what an achievement is. Most managers, when they become aware of an outstanding achievement by one of their subordinates, will try to recognize it. Managers are ready and willing to recognize those who win races or scale the highest mountains; achievements that are clearly evident. But what about the numerous people in the organization who are failing by lesser amounts today than yesterday? For example, when someone who was always a day late in delivering something now delivers it only half a day late, he is achieving by improving his performance. Achievement occurs when someone who always wastes a dollar on something now wastes only 75¢, or when someone who makes everybody mad at him, now only makes half that many mad at him.

Managers confess to me they have difficulty identifying achievements that are occurrences of less failure compared to previous levels of failure. Some even confess they find it difficult to thank someone for a lesser degree of failure if that individual is still failing. They believe that recognizing improvements in failing is really condoning failing (a little amateur psychology gets in the way here). There are really two difficulties. The first difficulty is the managers' inability to view *degrees of less failure* as *achievement*. It is easy to see the winners. Secondly, when managers try to compliment degrees of less failure they don't know what to say without being sarcastic, misunderstood, or embarrassed. They also wonder what the good worker will think when the failing worker is seemingly thanked for failure. The solution is: *Don't thank people for failing; thank them for achieving more* (more about this later).

Most managers view *recognition of achievement* as hanging medals on those individuals who win the races. It is easy enough to hang medals on winners. In fact there are winners in the business world who will win in spite of your helpful efforts (the high achievers). But management is not a function of playing head scorekeeper, where all you have to do is hang medals on the winners. Management is a function you perform to influence the outcome of the race. Management is recognizing those runners *during the race* who have never won, but have run the first hundred yards faster than they ever did before. That recognition will influence how they run the second hundred yards, and, eventually, will influence their position at the finish. The value of recognition as motivation is for managers to do everything possible during the race so twenty-seven people will tie for first. If, as Herzberg says, man is motivated by little bits of achievements that motivate him to try other little bits of achievement, managers should be recognizing degrees of less failure in their subordinates, and thereby motivating the subordinates to increase their efforts to fail by less.

Here is one manager's experience with recognizing achievement.

"The biggest changes occurred with one particular employee I had previously judged as uncooperative and antagonistic. Anytime he was given an assignment he would always botch it up in some way. Of course, he would also receive the wrath he deserved. His position in the company is such that I felt it would be worth the effort to try to make him more productive rather than terminating him and having to start from scratch with a new employee.

"My behavior changed in that I started to praise him for the right things he did after each assignment, making sure that I did so to a greater degree than when we discussed negative comments on things he did wrong. I also singled him out in front of others to praise him so that the rest of the staff would be aware that he was not a total loser. In some instances I would pair him with a co-worker doing the identical job so that he would get immediate feedback as to how he was performing that particular job. I, myself, have taken time to walk over to his desk while he is in the midst of his work to see how he was doing and to compliment him. In the past I would always wait until he had finished his assignment before going over it with him. I find now by showing him more interest in his work and by the combination of praise and lack of negative comments, his productivity has risen drastically. The amount of errors has diminished and he is actually asking about new assignments. There is still a lot of room for this individual's improvement but I now have him heading in the right direction."

If achievement and recognition are the single strongest motivators, the things you should do as a manager to increase productivity are as follows:

1. Get out from behind your desk so you can discover more incidents of achievement.
2. Be sure to recognize achievement when you become aware of it.
3. Interpret incidents of *lesser degrees of failure* as achievements; recognize them.
4. Make up a list of how many hundred ways you can make sounds come out of your mouth to show appreciation.

5. Write the initials of each person answering to you on your calendar each day. Then each day before you go home, put an *x* beside each one who achieved something and circle each *x* if you have recognized that achievement. Then do more of 1, 2, and 3 above to increase the number of *x*'s and circles.

PEOPLE ARE DIFFERENT—BUT DOES IT MATTER IN BUSINESS?

One theoretical obstacle to managers carrying out the face-to-face process is the invariable admonition they get from books and seminars that they recognize each of their subordinates as being different and that they treat them as individuals according to their differences. This is usually supported with detailed explanations of the personality anomalies throughout the population. It is assumed that knowledge of these anomalies will equip managers to identify individual personality differences and, therefore, to adapt their management efforts accordingly. This seems logical in view of all the literature describing the psychological complexities of man, but it leaves me with the important question, "Do managers have to understand as much about people as psychologists do, to successfully manage them in business?" This seems like an important question to me because if the answer is *yes* the next question is even tougher to answer: "How the hell do they do that without getting their Ph.D. in psychology?"

Let's explore this question to determine whether managers really have to do something they are not able to do, to become successful. Let's determine whether managers are faced with the same problems psychologists are faced with. For example, visualize a large office building with 2,000 people in it. Let's make believe you and I could somehow get those 2,000 people to exit the building, one at a time, through the same door, at sunset when it is getting a little difficult to see. Meanwhile you and I will hide behind a bush or a parked car very close to the exit they will be using. As each person comes out the door one at a time, you and I jump out from our hiding place and yell, "Stick 'em up!"

Now if we did that to each of the 2,000 people, do you think we would get 2,000 *different* reactions? The answer, of course, is no. Some individuals will faint, some will hand over their cash, some will cry, some will run away, some will fight, and some will wet their pants. Of course, there would be some combinations of reactions such as handing over the cash and wetting the pants, or throwing a punch and wetting the pants, etc. There might be twenty-five or thirty different reactions, but there would not be 2,000. Why not? If everyone is different why aren't there 2,000 different reactions?

You probably have guessed the answer already: *there are not 2,000 possible alternative reactions.* Because you and I restricted the parameters of the situation, we restricted the number of possible alternative actions. If we had held up 2,000 people (one at a time) in a phone booth, there would have been even fewer alternative actions available to them.

Let's go one step further; we will take these same 2,000 people, select a dozen at a time and place them in a lifeboat somewhere in the Caribbean. We make believe their cruise ship has just sunk. Some of them have to row, someone has to steer, someone has to fish, someone has to catch rain water, and someone has to hit sea gulls on the head. After you get everything settled down, someone jumps up, says, "I want to dance," and proceeds to do so.

Now what are you going to do? Are you going to sit this person down and try to get to know him better by talking about his previous life and work experience? Are you going to discuss family background, whether he loved mom or dad the best, what his brothers and sisters were like, whether he had a lot of toys to play with? Are you going to learn what his disappointments were in life, his achievements, and life's aspirations? Or will you most likely point out that the individual can row, steer, fish, hit sea gulls on the head, or catch rain water, but dancing is not an alternative?

Let's assume you do either, but the individual responds by saying, "I just want to dance," and continues to do so. Will you talk more about the individual's life and ambitions or will you say, "You can do any of the things I mentioned previously, but dancing is not an alternative; if you don't stop dancing we are either going to throw you overboard or tie you up and put you in the bottom of the boat and eat you for lunch."?

In a lifeboat situation the participants have limited alternatives of appropriate behavior available to them. If one persists in inappropriate behavior it is most likely self-destructive to themselves and the group. The captain or leader is left with few alternatives.

This example is used because there is considerable similarity between *business* and a *lifeboat*. There is no business that has its name written in the sky by the hand of any god that says, "This business will be here forever, no matter what it does." The opposite is true, "A business will be there only as long as it continues to do those things necessary for survival." Every year companies that someone assumed *would be here forever* fail.

The reason is that these companies ceased to do those things necessary for survival; they ceased to be profitable; they ceased to survive. Your company is a lifeboat; if everyone does not do the right things it will not survive. The division, department, or unit you manage is a lifeboat. If you and your subordinates don't do the right things you and they will not survive.

When psychologists think about man they consider what man is in the womb; they view man relative to his total environment, including parents, mate, and children; what he does when asleep and when awake; his life, loves, work, joys, and sorrows. The task of understanding the individual complexities of man is never ending for psychologists. Fortunately, managers are not faced with solving the same problems as the psychologists; that is trying to understand man as he relates to his total environment. Managers are faced only with the problem of managing human behavior in the restricted environment of the work situation, their lifeboat.

When a person seeking employment comes to your company and says, "I would like to come into your company," he is really saying, "I would like to come into your lifeboat." The implied agreement (written or not) goes something like this:

He: I will do what you tell me to do as long as you pay me with a check that doesn't bounce.

You: I will tell you what to do, give you some tools to do it with, and try not to dismember you in the process.

When you hire people as employees you do not buy people, or their bodies, or their brains, or their values. You merely rent their behavior. This might be broom-pushing behavior, typing behavior, drafting behavior, selling behavior, problem analysis behavior, idea-giving behavior, etc. Each job that must be done in your company is a collection of specific behaviors that, when done by the worker correctly, constitute that specific job. The opposite is also true. If a worker does not behave in a certain way, which constitutes a specific job, the worker is, in fact, not doing that job.

In business the appropriate behavior of any job is quite specific and limited. That is, if a worker behaves in certain ways, that behavior is appropriate, and if the worker behaves in certain other ways, that behavior is not appropriate. There is a major contrast between appropriate behavior in business jobs and appropriate behavior in other activities of life. There is a myriad of behaviors available to man throughout life that neither has constructive or destructive influences over his existence. In other words, there are numerous alternative behaviors available to man, most of which are appropriate. In business, however, in any specific job, the alternatives for appropriate behavior for that job are limited. There is not a wide choice of behavioral alternatives available to the worker if the job is to be done well.

When someone comes to work for your company, he is, in fact, offering to restrict his selection of alternative behaviors to those that you are willing to pay for. When one of your employees says, "I will not sweep the floor, I will not operate the computer console, I will not come to work on time, I will not complete my reports on time, I will not call on new customers," he is saying, to you "I WANT TO DANCE." He is saying "I refuse to give you the behavior I previously offered to rent to you." Now if employees refuse to behave in those specific ways required of that specific job, they are involved in SELF-DESTRUCTIVE BEHAVIOR. If the success of your unit depends on their behavior to survive, their inappropriate behavior is destructive to your unit. If you can't get them to stop their self-destructive behavior, you are involved in SELF-DESTRUCTIVE BEHAVIOR. The survival of your lifeboat (your unit) is at stake, and you, as the captain, are in equal danger of survival.

Another dramatic aspect of this relationship, which escapes most managers, is that when your subordinate does not do one or more of those things he is supposed to do, you, the manager, are automatically limited as to the alternative actions available to you related to that subordinate. Their inappropriate actions limit your actions; they have your back to the wall.

One management fallacy is the belief that managers have a complete freedom of action. Not only is each management job composed of specific appropriate behaviors, just like any other job, but the higher the level the job is, the less freedom of action there is. Even more important, the behavior of subordinates has a direct influence over the alternative behaviors of the manager. When subordinates do what they are supposed to do the manager has available a normal spectrum of alternative behavior. When a subordinate says, "I ain't gonna do it," the manager's alternatives become limited by the subordinate's behavior; the manager's behavior must be directed to dealing with that nonperformance.

In conclusion, although people are different, managers need not deal with that fact in the same way psychologists do. The manager's job is not managing people, but managing people's behavior within the restricted parameters of the business environment, which is significantly more restrictive than man's total aspect of life. When people accept employment in your company they choose to give up the privilege of behaving as differently as they might, because they choose to rent the specific behavior you will pay for. The behaviors that are appropriate in any job are quite specific. The survival of employees (in that job), your unit, you, and your company depends upon employees doing those things necessary for survival. When a subordinate does not do what he is supposed to do he is involved in self-destructive behavior. If he doesn't stop it, his behavior limits the alternatives available to you, their manager. His behavior dictates your behavior. If you can't get him to stop it, you are involved in self-destructive behavior.

This is not a brand new theory or another exciting bit of management buzz wordism; it just happens to be the plain facts about a simple relationship we have made complicated beyond recognition and control. You might say, "That sounds like a practical understanding of the relationship, but most employees don't see it that way."

Of course you are right; most employees don't see it that way. The reason they don't is because few of us make the effort to explain the facts of business life to them. People are hired in business to do jobs only because we don't have a machine that can do those jobs. You might say that people are doing jobs machines should be doing, but the machine has not yet arrived. In business a machine performs a profitable function when the results of what the machine does exceeds the cost of maintaining and operating that machine. The same relationship holds true of a worker. Any business resource must make a contribution to the business greater than the cost of maintaining that resource. The point at which a worker is paid exactly what he is worth is the point when that worker is no longer making a profitable contribution to that business. When the costs of maintaining a worker equal the value of the contribution the worker makes to the business, that relationship becomes a charitable relationship.

If you want the majority of employees in your business to understand the profit and loss aspects of business survival and the practical relationship of workers to work, teach them about profit and loss. Why should the words *Profit and Loss* be heard only in the executive wing or the accounting department? Tell people when you hire them that you are only renting their behavior, not purchasing their bodies and souls; then concentrate on managing people's behavior, not managing people.

4
An Alternative To Psychotherapy

The vast majority of the theoretical people management techniques taught to managers are based on the psychodynamic approach. This approach assumes that man is an inert organism and moves only when pushed or pulled by needs or drives.

Managers are taught that if you want to understand why people do things you must first understand their MOTIVES. And further, if you want people to behave differently you must first change their motives; the assumed result will be a change in their behavior. As previously mentioned, this places managers in the position of playing *amateur psychologist*. Happily for all you managers out there, there is another alternative. Part of this alternative comes from George A. Kelly, Ph.D., who was a professor and director of clinical psychology at The Ohio State University for twenty years.

According to Kelly, we need a theory about motives to explain why man moves only if we believe that man is inert. If we believe that man is *active* by the very nature of the fact that he is alive, we do not need a theory to explain why man moves because he is active and moving all the time. In his paper, "Man's Construction of His Alternatives,"[1] Kelly described some of his experiences as part of a travelling psychological clinic servicing schools in Kansas. He related how when a teacher complained that a pupil was lazy, he would proceed to

---

[1]Brendan Maher, *Clinical Psychology and Personality: The Selected Papers of George Kelly* (New York: John Wiley & Sons, 1969).

48

diagnose whether the child was lazy or was not lazy. If they worked at it long enough they could usually find *some grounds* to justify any teacher's complaint. But eventually Kelly discovered something he called *the law of the excluded middle*. This law implies that once you give a name to something, the only two alternatives available are *it is or it isn't* what you have named it. When a teacher called a pupil *lazy*, the only alternatives to the diagnostician was to find whether the child was *lazy* or *not lazy*. Kelly said, "When the teacher called a pupil lazy, we looked at the pupil as if it was so. But it was the teacher who called the pupil lazy, not the pupil."

To paraphrase one of his examples, let's suppose you and I were in a room full of people and I pointed to your left shoe and said *it is an introvert*. Because I have called the shoe an introvert the assumption is that somehow the shoe is responsible for it. We may even try to look closer to be sure whether it is or is not an introvert, when, in actual fact, introversion may not be an appropriate description for describing what your left shoe is. Since I called your shoe an introvert why do we look at the shoe rather than at me? It is I who placed the label of introversion on the shoe; why do we assume that because I say it *that makes it so*.

The importance of this concept to managers is the realization that labeling people because of what they do does not necessarily make them what we call them. Even more important to managers is the realization that *labeling* leads away from problem solutions rather than to them. For example, managers see problem behavior and label the worker (lazy is a good example). What happens in the real world is that we observe people who are not doing what we think they should be doing and, because it is clear to us that the worker knows there is something he should be doing, the obvious reason for the *not doing* is he is "*lazy*". We construe laziness as a kind of malady that certain people suffer from either because they were born that way or because of a certain sociological influence. Because we managers have labeled the worker, that label becomes the accepted cause of the problem behavior. Now that the subordinate has been labeled *lazy*, we can understand laziness as the reason for the *nonperformance*.

Kelly's next important observations came when he talked to pupils identified by their teacher as *uncooperative*. He frequently found the pupils had no idea they were being *uncooperative*. In fact, he found they were doing what they thought was perfectly logical to them at that time.

Kelly observed that man is an active organism, always in motion, always taking action. Because man is an active organism he is always faced with choosing alternative actions from those alternatives he sees available to him. Kelly describes how people view the world through their personal construct system. Each man views the world, the good, the bad, the happy, the unhappy on an individual basis. The assumption is that man will select what he believes to be the best alternative for him, from those alternatives he sees available at that time.

The implication from the above is that people do not go through the world doing *illogical things* on purpose. They do what they believe to be the right thing at that moment in time. They have selected (they believe) the best alternatives for them, from those alternatives they see available to them. What they do appears illogical to them only when they find out it didn't work. It appears illogical to someone else who is watching because that someone else sees more alternatives, or knows the one selected will not work.

Did you know that every year between 60 and 70 percent of the murders in this country do not occur in bank holdups, hijackings, and street corner muggings? They are not committed by criminals. They occur between best friends, relatives, loved ones, and next-door neighbors. When you ask Charlie why he stuck that butcher knife in his mother-in-law's throat, he says, "I had to shut her up and it seemed like a good idea at the time." To those of us not involved, that seems illogical. Perhaps if we talk to Charlie sitting in his cell waiting for sentencing, he also may agree that it was illogical (in retrospect). Perhaps if you or I were there when Charlie picked up the knife, we could have grabbed his wrist and said, "Do you realize you might get life for this or not get out of prison until you are sixty-seven; is there anything else you could do to shut her up?" Charlie then might have dropped the knife and punched his mother-in-law in the mouth.

If we believe man is an active organism, and we view man's actions as a continuous process of *selection of alternatives*, we quickly realize that experience is merely ADDING TO THE NUMBER OF ALTERNATIVES AN INDIVIDUAL HAS TO SELECT FROM, WHEN FACED WITH A DECISION OR ACTION (ALTER-NATIVE SELECTION).

For example, when you were seven years old and faced with a situation requiring a decision or action, you might have had only two alternatives to select from. They both may have been bad alternatives. If you were later faced with the same problem at age twelve, you might have had seventeen alternatives to select from. Your experience increased the number of alternatives to select from to solve the problem. It is likely that some of those seventeen alternatives were better than the two you had when you were seven.

Let's relate this to your work experience. Was there ever a time when you were stumped with a technical problem, couldn't land a sale, or couldn't handle a people management problem, and you went to your boss and said, "I tried A, B, and C but I just don't know how to solve this problem."? Your boss responded with "Why don't you try E?" and gave you a workable solution. Your response might be, "Why didn't I think of that?" The fact is that no matter how many alternative solutions you had, your boss needed only *one more* to help you solve your problem. He might have had thirty-five more alternatives to choose from.

There is no mystery or magic in experience. The function of experience is merely the act of adding to the number of alternatives you have to select from, when you are required to act. This means that when you point to someone and say, "She does not have enough experience to do that," you are really saying, "That person does not have enough alternatives to choose from when required to act in that situation." In business the problem *needs more experience* is too frequently solved through the equivalent of making someone do something for *more years*, when the actual learning (acquiring additional alternatives) could have been accomplished in two weeks. Therefore, the solution to the *not enough experience* problem is not to require the individual to live more days, weeks, or years in that work situation, but to help them acquire those additional alternatives that are needed. If you know what those alternatives are, you can solve the problem by giving them to the worker.

What this means to you as a manager is that there is an alternative to the requirement that you become a psychologist before you become a successful manager. That alternative is to forget about people's motives; you don't know for sure what they are anyhow. If you want to know why people do things, try to understand the practical alternatives they were confronted with, and ask them why they selected the alternatives they did. Recognize that a person's behavior takes place within the dimensions of his own personal construct system, his own view of the good, the bad, the hurt, and the happiness in the world. Stop interpreting the actions of your workers in view of the alternatives *you see* available to them. Interpret what they do in view of the alternatives *they see* available to them. THEY DO NOT SEE THE ALTERNATIVES THAT YOU SEE AVAILABLE.

If you want them to select better alternatives, give them more alternatives to select from, or let them know now the future consequence of the alternatives they are selecting.

ATTITUDE—A BARRIER TO EFFECTIVE MANAGEMENT

How many times have you felt you knew what people's attitudes were? How many times have you interpreted a worker's good or poor performance as related to his attitudes? Do you assume that people do good work because of good (or positive) attitudes and poor work because of poor (or negative) attitudes? Therefore, do you believe that when you change their attitudes they will do better work? Have you ever criticized a subordinate's unsatisfactory work performance, stating the reason for the poor performance as his poor or negative attitude, and pointed out that the solution to solving the performance problem was for the individual to change his attitude?

If you are similar to 90 percent of the managers out there in the world, you will admit to all or part of the above. Most managers I have taught or worked with in the last fifteen years have readily admitted to the same. Once managers tell me they know their subordinates' attitudes (even sometimes) I ask them how they know. The answers are always the same:

1. I see what they do (their actions, nonactions, reactions, achievements.
2. They tell me.
3. Self yardstick (I did that and I know what my attitude was, so they must feel the same way.

Some managers say they know what people's attitudes are because *other people* tell them, but the only method the *other people* actually have is one or all of the above.

Next, I ask them: "What is attitude?" The answer to this usually requires a lengthy discussion because most people have difficulty defining *attitude*, although they freely talk about it. Finally, we end up with something like this:

"Attitude is how people feel about themselves and the world around them, and can include quite specific feelings or values, such as likes and dislikes."

After we have defined attitude, I ask: "Where does attitude occur?" The unanimous answer is "in the person's head" or "between the ears." Then I ask them to explain to me how they actually use the three sources of information given above to determine what people's attitudes are.

For example, "If attitude occurs between people's ears, tell me how your observations of the things they do (their actions) lets you know what is occurring between their ears?" This usually leads to a long discussion of people's stereotyped behavior and the supposition that certain attitudes are unalterably linked to certain behavior, i.e., "People do best what they like and do poorly what they don't like." It takes effort to get managers to admit that they do things everyday they don't like to do or don't want to do but they do them anyhow and do them well. Therefore, if you and I saw them doing those things we might assume they loved doing those things.

As the discussion progresses managers admit there is something in life they used to like to do and did well, but they have done it so frequently they no longer like to do it; still they have to do it well and they do. They also admit there is something in life they didn't like to do but had to do, and now, because they have done it so much, they have begun to like it. The realization slowly becomes accepted that there is no permanent link between any specific attitude and any specific action. It is quite possible for people to do something five times in a row but have five changes in attitudes in relation to that thing.

Eventually managers admit they do not know what a person's attitude is by observing behavior. Of course they are right. What they are really doing is observing someone's behavior and guessing about the attitude that is occurring between that person's ears as related to their behavior. Still, they hasten to add that their guesses get better the longer they do it. "It is difficult," they say, "to know if any specific guess is right or wrong, but over a period of time your guesses will improve." This is ridiculous. If you observe a subordinate's behavior and make guesses about the attitude connected with that behavior over a five-year period some of your guesses will be right and some of your guesses will be wrong. The real problem is: HOW WILL YOU KNOW WHICH OF YOUR GUESSES WERE RIGHT AND WHICH OF YOUR GUESSES WERE WRONG?

For example, let's suppose you and I are face to face, and I ask you to guess how much change I have in my pocket. I will shake my pocket to let you hear what it sounds like. After you guess I say, "Well, isn't that interesting," and walk away, depriving you of knowing how much change there really is in my pocket. How would you know whether your guess was right or wrong? Your single guess has not been verified. It may have been correct, but without verification you would not know whether it was or not.

You may complain that this example is unrealistic because the guesses you make about your subordinates' attitudes are more numerous and occur over a longer period of time. You believe that your guesses will improve over time. It will be more reasonable to let you make 2,000 guesses as to how much change is in my pocket. I will shake my pocket each time to give you some behavior to observe. Because you are clever, you will also record my reactions each time you make a guess (did I smile, or frown, or shift from one foot to the other, or slump my shoulders, etc.). At the end of your 2,000 guesses you will analyze your data and relate my smiles, frowns, and body posture to the amounts you guessed. Clever as you are, you will surmise that certain of my reactions were related to a correct guess. For example, it may appear obvious to you that I smiled when you were incorrect and frowned when you were correct. You will probably isolate those guesses that appear to correspond with those reactions. But, after you have analyzed all the information you have collected and make your final best guess, I say, "Well, isn't that interesting," and walk away without telling you the true amount of the change in my pocket. Again you are without verification whether your guess was correct or even close. There is no question that many of your 2,000 guesses would be correct. Many of them would also be wrong. The critical question again is: "How will you know which of your guesses are right and which are wrong, if your guesses are never verified?"

When managers realize that number one above, as a method for knowing what people's attitudes are, is really *guessing*, they agree that guessing is not an effective or businesslike basis for identifying people's attitudes. But they quickly go on to number 2, *I know what their attitudes are because they tell me.* This sounds like pretty firm ground, but it presents two problems. The first problem is related to the fact that *we do not always know what our attitudes are, even though we say we do.* Research has demonstrated that people frequently do things that are in contrast with what they state to be their attitudes. When this contradiction is shown to them they often restate their attitudes. We are not our own psychotherapists. What we talk about as being important to us frequently is not what is really important to us. I, for example, drive an economy car for the obvious reason that it is economical to operate. It is a Mercedes diesel. Diesel fuel costs about 5¢ less than gasoline. If you talk to the dealer who sold me my car, and tell him what I believe about my economy car, he will probably laugh and suggest that I would have to drive a lot of miles to make up in fuel savings the added cost of a $35,000 car. But I believe I know why I drive it regardless of what he says. The fact is that people do not always know what their attitudes are even though they say they do. Therefore, when someone tells you what his attitude is, how do you know he knows what it is?

The second problem we face is that even if the individual knew what his attitude was, how do we know he is telling the truth? Strange as it may seem, patients lie even to their own psychotherapist, or tell them WHAT THEY THINK THEY WANT TO HEAR, even though the patient went there for healing purposes. So why in the world would you expect anyone to be totally truthful to you, his boss, who wields power over his destiny?

How many times have you heard managers say, "I think my subordinates only tell me what they think I want to hear"? There is a lot of truth in that statement. Sometimes managers respond by stating they believe their people are honest with them. Usually I ask them if they are honest in their dealings with the people they work with and the answer is *yes*. Then I ask them if they ever have to deal with someone they dislike, and would it be self-destructive if that person discovered the manager disliked him. The answer is usually *yes*. Then I ask them what they would do if that person asked them, "Do you dislike me?" The answer invariably is: "I would say no."

In the real world, people must sustain numerous relationships with other people. In the interest of preserving those relationships, people tend to say what they believe to be appropriate, rather than what they actually think. These decisions to say one thing rather than another during the numerous interactions are considered a social grace rather than lying. In a boss-subordinate relationship, it might be considered self-preservation. It is usually easy to get managers to recognize that number 2 above is not a practical or businesslike basis for knowing people's attitudes.

This leaves the third basis for knowing what people's attitudes are: *I used to do that and I know how I felt about it, so they must feel the same way.* Some managers are quick to recognize: *if I just learned that I don't always know what my attitudes are, then I can't very well do this.* Of course they are right, but even if you were certain of your own attitudes, I would have to ask you, "Who registered you in Washington with the National Bureau of Standards as having the 'normal' attitudes for humanity or for anyone?" As a matter of fact, if you are a successful manager you probably do not have normal attitudes. To be a successful manager (at least in this country) you have to be a high achiever. The higher you go up the management ladder, the greater is the requirement you be a high achiever to get there.

Let's look at the difference between high achievers and normal people. The normal people come to work on time and leave work on time; sometimes they arrive early and sometimes they work late. They hurry home to spend time with their families, Little League sports, civic activities, hobbies, etc. The high achievers come to work early most of the time and stay late most of the time. They work until 6, 7, 8, 9, and 10:00 o'clock at night, six or seven days a week. The average work week of a high level executive varies from 60 to 90 hours. Their luncheon and dinner engagements are with business people for business reasons. Their golf, tennis, or handball games are with business people for business reasons. Even vacations are scheduled at times and places where business can be combined with pleasure. For example, a two-week vacation with the family is spent in Spain because the company's plant there can be visited at the same time. If a high achiever were going to visit a hospitalized spouse or friend but received a call about a business problem that just came up in Chicago, the high achiever would most likely send flowers to the hospital and catch a plane to Chicago.

We high achievers are not normal; we are a little neurotic, but we do not want to be changed. The life of a high achiever can be very satisfying. We try a lot of things and we accomplish a lot of things. We work hard at what we do, and we win a lot. When we win a lot in the business world, it usually means we make a lot of money that can buy a lot of tangible benefits. Most of us high achievers got where we are with little help from others. Frequently we achieved despite the helpful efforts from others, including our bosses.

The first mistake we high achievers make after we get knighted as managers, is in how we classify the people who work for us. If we are lucky enough to hire a high achiever, our first reaction is to say to ourselves, "Wow, I finally acquired a normal person; someone who believes in the protestant ethic; someone who understands the agony of defeat and the ecstasy of success." We may even go home at night and pray to our favorite deity, "Thank you, God, for sending me a normal person like me. If you get a chance will you send me a couple more normal people, and help me get rid of those subnormal goofoffs who can't accomplish anything without looking over their shoulder all the time." It seems logical that we should compare the people who work for us to what we think we know best—ourselves. Unfortunately, we assume we are normal. We should really be praying like this: "Dear God, thank you for sending me a high achiever. If you get a chance could you please send me a few more neurotics like me? But please give me the knowledge, understanding, and strength to do what they pay me to do, which is to manage those normal people to help them be as successful as possible." Because we high achievers were successful without assistance, or in spite of it, we assume that is the only way it should be, and we perceive our management job as *pointing high achievers in the right direction and whispering in their ears, "Go get 'em!"*

In two studies I made of performance-appraisal programs in American and Canadian companies I frequently found statements like these on their appraisal forms:

"Does the individual do that little bit more, or only what's expected?"

"Is this person able to work effectively with minimum supervision?"

The first statement, which was used to identify a normal performer, assumes that if the individual is a normal performer (a high achiever like us), he or she will always do more than what is expected. Have you ever heard a manager say, "If I have to tell them what to do, they are wrong for the job."? This also means, "He who does only what is expected is a below-normal performer."

The second statement was also used to identify *good* or *normal* performance. What is most interesting is there was no corresponding statement, such as "Is this person able to work effectively with normal supervision?". The underlying assumption is that the normal manager-subordinate relationship is one of only minimum supervision. This means that any amount of supervision more than minimum (whatever that is) is indicative of poor worker performance. But in the real world managers don't get paid for *minimum supervision*; they get paid for *maximum supervision*, whatever is necessary to achieve results. Managers must construe supervision as those things a manager does to guide, help, and support the success of subordinates, and they must recognize that managers don't get paid for minimum effort, but for maximum effort to achieve results. The only reason you are there as a manager is to do everything possible to help your subordinates to be as successful as possible.

Not only is point number 3, *self yardstick*, just as fallacious as the other two as a basis for knowing people's attitudes, but if you use it, you will expect your subordinates to perform just like you, with minimum assistance. Therefore, they will be deprived of the help they need to be successful, and you will be involved in self-destructive behavior.

So, the only conclusion left is WE REALLY DON'T KNOW WHAT PEOPLE'S ATTITUDES ARE. We only guess at what they are and then become trapped into believing our guesses are correct. The insidious part of this self-delusion is that once you believe you know what a subordinate's attitude is, you then believe you can blame that bad or negative attitude for causing poor performance. Since it is the worker's attitude that is wrong, it is the worker who must change it. Your only alternative is to tell them they must change it, and step back to keep score whether or not they do it. Since it is obviously the worker's fault and the worker must correct it, you just put yourself out of the management of that human resource.

There is another trap for you when you believe you know what people's attitudes are. If you really believe you are able to know what people's attitudes are, then you are in the *mind-reading business*. If you believe you are able to read minds when talking to other people you are really talking to yourself. What you do is project your thoughts into somebody else's head and then direct your conversation to those thoughts you obviously know are there; you are talking to yourself. A sure sign that you are doing this is when the person you are talking to is acting in ways that are not related to what you are talking about. The problem is that you are not responding to his communication signals; you are holding both sides of the conversation in your own head.

If you finally recognize that you can't read minds, you will find yourself somewhat alone in the world because everybody else believes they are able to do it. For example, an article written by an associate professor of psychology recently appeared in the journal of a guidance counselors' professional organization. It started like this:

"All counselors use extrasensory perception (ESP) and experience residing beyond the ordinary senses without even realizing it."

"How many times have counselors looked at their clients and immediately had distinct feelings about them? These feelings can be a form of ESP."

Of course there have been numerous times when we all have looked at other people and immediately had distinct feelings about them. But our feelings tell us what is going on inside our head, not what is going on inside their heads. If you believe you know what is going on inside somebody else's head, you know you are right, *because you know you are right*; no one can prove you are wrong. Even if the other person claims what you believe about him is incorrect, you still know you are right; he simply will not admit it.

It is unfortunate for both the manager and the subordinate if the manager believes he or she has some undefined powers to assist in the management process. But for professionals, schooled in the people-helping professions, to believe they have undefined powers to assist them is not only ludicrous, it is tragic.

I have been in the people management business for twenty years, and I discovered nineteen and a half years ago that I couldn't read minds. My best advice to you as a manager is to get out of the mind-reading business. The necessity for you to be a successful people manager is too important to you to base it on mysticism.

I realize it is not easy for you to give up something that is such a familiar part of our way of life; everybody talks about everybody else's attitude. When a waitress places a plate noisily on your table in a restaurant, the natural response is to comment about her poor attitude. You do not know whether the plate was greasy, her arthritis was acting up, or her doctor called to tell her the rabbit test was positive. In this casual situation there is no harmful consequence to you in playing the attitude game. Your choice will be to leave a smaller tip, which leaves more money in your pocket. It doesn't make any difference to you what the real reason was for the sloppy service. To play the *Attitude-Guessing Game* as a manager, however, is *self-destructive behavior.*

5
A Theory You Can
Put To Practical Use

As mentioned earlier, the predominant management training in the people management process uses the internalized theories as a basis to describe why people do things, i.e., people do things because of their inner drives, motives, and attitudes. Happily, there is another alternative, the scientific perspective of human behavior called *behaviorism*. This scientifically derived body of knowledge is based on the premise that *all behavior is a function of its consequences.* Specifically translated, it means that people do the things they do because of the results or consequences to them. This scientific approach to people management, sometimes called *behavior modification*, has demonstrated that not only can people's behavior be changed regardless of what their attitudes might be, but, once the behavior has been changed, the attitude usually follows (if you care to know about the attitude).

Behavioral science as a conceptual approach to understanding why people do things is perhaps seventy years old. Behavior modification, as a scientific practice of changing or directing the behavior of people as therapy, training, or management practice, has made quantum jumps in acceptance in the last fifteen years. If you feel the word *scientific* is heavily used here, you are right. Behavior modification deals only with measurable behavior, in contrast to the theoretical, internalized activities of man's mind, which are not measurable.

The behaviorists tell us that for every action there are two possible consequences to the individual; there could be a positive consequence and there could be a negative consequence. One primary rule of the behavior modification concept, which is most meaningful to you, is as follows:

Behavior that is followed by a positive consequence (to the individual behaving) will tend to repeat itself.

As an example let's take a look at how the action of mowing the lawn might look in this concept.

MOWING THE LAWN TODAY

Positive Consequences
1. Lawn looks nice
2. Easier to do because grass is not too long
3. Neighbors tell you how nice it looks

Negative Consequences
1. Don't play golf today
2. Perspire in hot sun
3. Physical effort

NOT MOWING THE LAWN TODAY

Positive Consequences
1. Play golf
2. No perspiration
3. No physical effort

Negative Consequences
1. Lawn looks terrible
2. Grass too long next weekend— hard to cut
3. Neighbors make snide remarks about lawn

Although this is a very simple analysis of some of the possible alternative consequences to doing or not doing something called *mowing the lawn*, it can be easily seen how the positive consequence for not mowing the lawn might result in some very long grass.

If you accept the fact that people do the things they do because of the consequences of what they do, it is easy to understand why people will increase the frequency of doing something if each time they do it, a positive consequence usually results. Quite frankly, if you do something and the result is a pleasant experience to you, isn't it likely you are going to do that something again? The idea is simple enough to grasp, but there are some nuances that must be explained. For example, when a person does something there can be many consequences: short-range consequences, long range consequences, consequences to them, consequences to people around them, and also negative consequences or painful events. The principle described above works if:

1. The consequence is to the individual.
2. The consequence is positive.
3. The consequence occurs soon after the action.

The second rule, which is important for you to understand, is:

Any consequence that occurs after an action and increases the frequency of that action is called a positive reinforcer.

For example, if you give jelly beans, hugs and kisses, or gold stars to people after they do a certain thing, and the frequency of that thing increases, the jelly beans, hugs and kisses, and gold stars are *positive reinforcers*. More specifically, we could make some pretty good guesses that under certain conditions jelly beans, hugs and kisses, and gold stars are considered positive consequences by the individuals acting. We can know for sure whether or not these are positive reinforcers only if the frequency of behavior we are reinforcing increases.

Let's look at the possible ways positive consequences of an action may influence that action. For example, let's say I have a four-year-old daughter who I am encouraging to practice the social amenities. Let's assume I am now standing in a room full of guests and I say to my daughter, "Tondalayo, be a good little girl and say hello to everybody." I accompany this with a gentle shove from behind to initiate Tondalayo's movement into the room. Tondalayo takes the necessary steps to maintain her balance, looks around the room, begins to cry, and rushes to me, burying her head on my knee. My reaction is to bend down and stroke Tondalayo's head, hug and kiss her, and, perhaps, give her candy or ice cream.

Let me ask you: "Did Tondalayo do what I wanted her to do?" The answer is obviously no. What consequence followed that *not doing*? Was it a positive consequence or a negative consequence to Tondalayo? We probably would be safe in assuming that the hugging and kissing and candy or ice cream were positive consequences to her.

I am concerned about my daughter learning the social amenities. If I use my typical amateur psychological approach, I might try to converse with her asking why didn't she socialize, what is she afraid of, and I might explain the importance of her socializing and how she must grow up to be a socially oriented person. But I know in advance that my chances of holding such a discussion will not be successful with my four-year old daughter, so I turn to the behaviorist

and ask: "What can I do to get my daughter to do more social things?"
The behaviorist's first response is likely to be: "Stop rewarding her for
not doing what you want her to do." And the conversation might go
something like this.

Me: But after all she was crying.
Behaviorist: Does she cry a lot?
Me: Yes.
Behaviorist: Do you hug and kiss her everytime she cries?
Me: Yes.
Behaviorist: Looks like Tondalayo is controlling your behavior. It
appears that Tondalayo has learned that good things
can be made to happen by crying. If you want to
decrease her frequency of crying, one way is to stop
rewarding it.
Me: You mean when I ask her to say hello to friends and
she cries and hugs my leg, I should remove the positive
consequences of kissing and hugging?
Behaviorist: Right. Do not reward her for nonperformance.
Me: When do I kiss and hug her?
Behaviorist: When her behavior approximates what you want. For
example, if she goes a longer period without crying, or
takes a step closer to your friends, or she smiles, or
talks, or touches them, then run up to her and hug and
kiss her.

The important point here for you to perceive is that although we both
thought I was being nice to my daughter in displaying parental love
and affection in her moment of frustration, what I was actually doing
was rewarding her for not performing. Now if I, in fact, did ignore
Tondalayo's nonperforming behavior (crying and not being social),
and I hugged and kissed her when I saw the behavior I did want (longer
periods without crying, talking, etc.), we would expect to see an
increase in the desired behavior. The periods of not crying would get
longer and the incidents of talking would increase.

If you take a minute to think about it I am sure you could name
many situations in life where positive consequences are reinforcing
people's actions. For example, in our modern society, at least here in
the United States, half of the population successfully manages the

behavior of the other half. As an example let me ask you this question: "When a man is pressuring a woman what does the man do when the woman cries?" You are right. He usually stops pressuring the woman. The consequence to the woman who is crying is that pressure goes away because of crying behavior. To the man who is pressuring the woman the positive consequence of removing the pressure is that the crying behavior stops. This crying behavior, which is predominant in females, is a learned response rather than inborn. At very early ages both male and female children are quite successful in using crying behavior to bring about positive consequences. When boys and girls reach a certain age, however, the boy is usually punished for crying behavior, but the girl isn't. As further growth continues there are social influences that decrease crying in boys and permit it to increase in girls. For example, one of the positive consequences of a boy not crying in situations where he formerly did is to be recognized as a *brave little man*. The female's behavior continues to be reinforced; that is, her crying behavior brings positive consequences to her.

Another aspect of behavior modification deals with the negative consequences, or painful events, that occur following an action. One important principle that relates to negative consequence is:

Behavior that is followed by a negative consequence or a painful event will decrease in frequency.

In fact, the most effective method of decreasing the frequency of behavior is to administer punishment or painful events to the person behaving. But before you say, "Aha, I always knew that," let me tell you something else. There are several aspects of the administering of painful events to decrease a behavior frequency that create more problems than benefits.

One of the first problems in the administration of negative consequences or painful events is that the person handing out these consequences often misinterprets what is, and what is not a negative consequence. For example, have you ever witnessed a situation where a child was misbehaving on purpose, with the result that the child received some kind of physical punishment or chastisement? Afterwards you or the other adults involved might have wondered why a child would appear to want to be punished. In the meantime the child may have walked away rubbing the spanked area, but thinking: "They still love me." As with positive consequences, a consequence is positive or negative only as interpreted by the receiver of that consequence. If love and attention are a positive consequence to a child and there isn't much of that happening, then any attention, even chastisement, may be a positive consequence to that child. Attention is a powerful reinforcer even if it is chastisement. So the first problem in using negative consequences or painful events to decrease the frequency of a behavior is that the negative consequence you are passing out may in fact be a positive consequence, and, therefore, will increase the frequency of the behavior you don't want.

The second aspect of using negative consequences is that it creates unwanted side effects. In situations where people receive negative consequences or painful events, they become apprehensive. Therefore, if your management style is typical of most managers, and you use negative consequences to change people's behavior, you will be dealing with very apprehensive people.

Another serious side effect to negative consequences is aggression. When people are subjected to punishment or painful events, they may decrease the frequency of the behavior that is causing the painful consequence, but they may also react aggressively by holding work back, causing disruptive actions, and even sabotaging work performance. When I ask managers, "Why don't subordinates do what they are supposed to do?", one answer that comes up fairly often is *because they don't like the boss*. When I get them to explain what they mean by that, they usually tell me that because the subordinate doesn't like the boss, he will foul up performance to injure the boss or his reputation. That, clearly, is an act of aggression by that subordinate. In other words, the positive consequences of not doing work as a worker is to get the boss in hot water. It is difficult enough for managers to manage the productivity of subordinates who are neutral at best. It becomes almost impossible if the subordinates are aggressively trying to achieve the downfall of the boss.

So, the most important observation we can make from these comments about the side effects of negative consequences and painful events is to avoid them whenever possible. Instead of directing your attention to decreasing the subordinates' behavior YOU DON'T WANT, direct your attention to increasing the subordinates' behavior YOU DO WANT.

Much of the work in behavior modification has been applied in educational situations. For example, one study found that one of the reasons students didn't do their homework was because of social rejection. Those who did their homework were labeled as eggheads. The long-range positive consequence to those children who did their homework was that they would get higher grades and do better at higher levels of education and, eventually, get into the college of their choice. Unfortunately, those long-range consequences are extremely difficult to perceive as a value to children in grade school. There was no immediate positive consequence to outweigh the immediate negative consequence of being labeled an egghead by peers. The action taken by the teacher was to advise the students that for every completed homework assignment, they were permitted to write their name on a sheet of paper and place it in a jar at the back of the room. At the end of each week one name would be drawn out of the jar and the student whose name was drawn would receive a prize (the value of the prize was under $2.00). By this action the teacher provided an immediate positive consequence for doing homework, which was more important than the negative consequence of peer pressure. As a result of this change, the number of children completing their homework assignments rose from less than a quarter of the class to almost two-thirds of the class in a sixty-day period. Please note that this is not an isolated circumstance that has occurred once in the last fifty years. This is an example of a common practice of providing an immediate positive consequence where none existed before, to increase the frequency of desired behavior.

Let's consider how consequences affect behavior in business. Every business has certain jobs that people don't do too well. These jobs may be considered tedious or very difficult or annoying to do. Think of one of these jobs in your own organization, and ask yourself what happens when a person does not do it well. If your organization is like most, the answer is, *you never ask them to do it again.* In other words the positive consequence for a worker who does a certain job poorly is that he is not asked to do that job again. When someone comes along who does that tedious or difficult or annoying job well, the boss's immediate response is to schedule all of the crummy work for that individual who does it so well. In other words, the consequence for doing that job well is, *You get to do that crummy work all the time.*

Let me ask you another question: When you have a critical task that must be done in a hurry, or without errors, etc., whom do you give it to? Do you give it to your subordinates who always do the best work, or to those who screw up occasionally? Most managers would consider that an easy choice. "I always give that priority work to my best workers." Sounds logical, doesn't it? But what you don't realize is that you are changing the behavior of the other workers, the *screw-ups*. They are learning, *the less I do around here, the less they ask me to do.* It is unlikely they will ever verbalize it, but that is what they are learning. Isn't that a nice positive consequence for nonperformance?

If you consistently load up the same people with the hot projects, three possible things generally occur: they get promoted; their level of performance begins to drop off; or they resign. If they do resign you naturally ask why they are leaving, and the answer is always *for more money*. This is why managers complain about not being able to pay their high performers enough to keep them. Unfortunately, managers are deluded because they don't ask the right questions. The fact is that almost everyone leaving your company for another job will be paid more in their new job. The same thing is true of the people your company hires; they will be paid more money working for you than on their last job. The new employer probably asked the right question, which is, "Why do you want to leave your job?" The most likely answer is, "The more you do over there, the more they ask you to do; there are people over there doing half as much work as I do and the managers don't ask them to do any more. I would like to work where the work is distributed fairly." This is not a fairy tale; this is what is happening out there when the consequences of doing a crummy job well is to get to do all the crummy work!

Now picture a manager who has an employee with an absentee problem. This manager has been exposed to the standard management training programs that lead her to believe she is capable of functioning as an amateur psychologist. Her first step to solve the absentee problem is to get to know the subordinate better. She calls the employee in, perhaps offers him a cup of coffee, and talks about the employee's background, the satisfactions and dissatisfactions in his life, and his future hopes and aspirations. They might discuss things the manager could do to make the company a better place to work, and she might even ask what job he would really like to have. The manager hopes that, as a result of this discussion, the employee will recognize the manager's interest and concern and will, therefore, be absent less. What is actually happening is that one of the consequences of absenteeism behavior is to get free coffee and to spend a lot of time sitting in the boss's office talking about yourself. What do you suppose the same manager does to all of those employees who come to work every day? Nothing. According to the manager's logic, nothing is required; they come to work every day.

If you have spent a considerable amount of time interviewing people for hire, you undoubtedly asked them how they were treated where they previously worked. If your experience is typical, one of the most common responses you would have gotten is, *The only time the boss talks to you over there is when you foul something up.* What this means from a behavioral point of view is that the consequence (a negative one) for doing everything you are supposed to do correctly is to be ignored by the boss.

Of course many managers tell me they don't buy coffee for their problem employees. They call them in and really make it hot for them, although the absentee problem doesn't get any better. It is inconceivable to them that their yelling, screaming, and threatening could be anything but a negative consequence to the subordinate. In school situations it frequently occurs that children who are yelled at by the teacher for pulling hair and throwing spit balls increase their frequency of hair pulling and spit ball throwing. This is mystifying to the teacher until she is helped to realize that her attention is a positive consequence to the child, and, because the misbehavior is increasing in frequency, her attention must be reinforcing it. The situation is usually corrected when the teacher ignores the behavior she does not want but gives her *attention* following behavior she does want. The result is a decrease in inattentive behavior and an increase in attentive behavior. It is important for managers to realize that whether they think a consequence is positive or negative is irrelevant; only the view of the individual receiving the consequence is relevant.

Not too long ago, a manager in one of my classes told me it appeared he had people working for him who seemed to do things wrong on purpose so they could confess it to him. He said, "It seemed they really wanted me to yell at them." The puzzle disappeared when he described his relationship with his subordinates in more detail. His subordinates were highly educated, technically oriented individuals who worked independently at a professional level. Because their responsibilities were clearly identified, everyone was expected to work relatively unsupervised. He went on to explain that because everybody was experienced and knew what he was supposed to do, his contacts with them were quite infrequent. Except for the planning meetings at the beginning of the year subsequent meetings occurred only when problems came up, and these meetings were usually initiated by the subordinates. Although the meetings were initiated to discuss problems, he described the meetings as very low key. It was usually a pleasant discussion with mutual agreement on solutions and both parties pleased at the outcome. I asked him: "Because your discussions throughout the year with your subordinates are infrequent, and you describe these problem-solving meetings as very pleasant discussions, is it possible your subordinates view these problem-solving discussions as a positive consequence?" His response was, "My God, am I one of those bosses who only talks to their subordinates when they screw up?" He was right.

Another illustration of the relationship between an individual's behavior and the consequences is apparent in the case of a sixteen-year-old girl who was a *thumb sucker*. If you were to use the internalized approach in an effort to determine the causes and possible solutions for a sixteen-year-old girl sucking her thumb, you might conjure up visions of childhood privation. Analysis of this *thumb sucking* in a behavior/consequence framework, however, determined that the only time this girl sucked her thumb was when her parents yelled at her. The mystery became even less mysterious when it was further learned that when she sucked her thumb, HER PARENTS STOPPED YELLING AT HER. *Thumb sucking* appeared to be a purely logical behavior on the part of this sixteen-year-old girl. If you want your parents to stop yelling at you, you stick your thumb in your mouth. What can be more practical than that? If the parents wanted the child to stop sucking her thumb, all they had to do was *stop yelling at her*.

A corollary to this in business might be the manager who is surprised and insulted when subordinates storm out of his office. He might not be so surprised if he were to learn that the only time his subordinates storm out of his office is when he yells at them. If he wants them to stop storming out of his office, the correct solution may be for him to change his behavior and talk to them rather than yell at them. Remember what we learned from the ideas of George Kelly? *People do not do illogical things on purpose. What they do appears perfectly logical to them at the time they are doing it.*

The process of behavior modification is much more scientific in practice, and involves more variables and techniques than presented here. It would be ridiculous of me, however, to convince you to stop being one type of amateur psychologist only to become another type of amateur psychologist. I don't plan to do that. The purpose of this book is to help you improve your face-to-face techniques to improve the productivity of your subordinates. The only way for you to be successful at that is to get out of the business of being any kind of amateur psychologist and manage the variables over which you have control.

Therefore, from a practical management view point, the only alternative to the psychodynamic approach is the management of behavior. Behavior is the only thing you can deal with. You can see it when it is bad, you can measure it, and you can talk about it unemotionally. You can see it when it changes, and you can measure it after it changes. If you separate yourself from the internalized reasons for behavior, and start dealing with that behavior itself, you will be able to separate people from their behavior. You will learn how appropriate it is to be able to say, "I like you very much, but I dislike your behavior. If you would change your behavior I would like it as much as I like you." And if you start trying to change behavior rather than trying to change people, you will no longer be faced with the resistance people naturally present, because *they don't want to be changed.*

Here is how one student manager described his experience using positive reinforcement.

My job function is to manage fifteen people whose jobs range from truck driver to clerk to office manager. Most of the time I do not get involved with the lower echelon, unless the office manager has a problem he can't solve. It so happened that he came to me about a particular problem he was having with a truck driver who was fast at his work, but who ignored the details. The manager explained that on numerous occasions he had instructed the driver to make sure he filled out his pick-up tags completely, but the driver was not responding to his request. Rather than try to explain to my manager what to do and how to do it, I decided to make the driver part of my class project.

I instructed my manager not to say anything further to the driver about the pick-up tags until I had a chance to talk to him. The next day as soon as the driver returned to the office from his morning rounds I immediately approached him and proceeded to compliment him on how well and how fast he was making his pick ups and deliveries. Ordinarily, the only time I would talk to the driver was to register some complaints, so it was easily understandable why he had a puzzled look on his face. After I complimented him, I suggested that he might try to fill out his pick-up tags completely, as this would facilitate the handling of the equipment and eliminate errors. The driver said he would fill out the tags completely. The next day I checked to see if he had performed his job correctly and he had. At this point I congratulated him for his improvement, and I followed up again in a few days. I found at this point that he was still doing his job correctly, whereupon I expressed my satisfaction and thanked him again for the fine job he was doing. My manager has not had any further problem with him along these lines. Badgering and threatening about the unsatisfactory performance did no good, whereas praise and recognition (positive reinforcement) for desired performance were the answer.

In addition to trying to solve specific problems I have consciously changed my behavior so as not to show any of my true feelings if I happen to be in a bad mood. In the morning I make a point of saying "good morning" to everyone on an individual basis, referring to each one by his name, rather than a quick general "good morning." I now also recognize everyone for the jobs they do by telling them how I appreciate their specific efforts. In the past *I would say nothing if they did their jobs the way they were supposed to do them.* I would pat them on the back only if they did an outstanding job.

I am pleased to report that the productivity of these people has increased noticeably, which was to me a nice surprise. I did not expect their productivity to go up because I felt they were producing at their maximum performance level over the long run. I felt that I could not ask them to produce more because I was satisfied with their work and I did not want to alienate them. Without asking them to do anything, just by changing my behavior, the average productivity of the employees has improved. I have noticed also that if the job is running past the 5:00 P.M. quitting time, some of the employees will remain a few extra minutes to complete their assignment. This free overtime never occurred in the past and I can only attribute it to the different way I am doing things.

As a manager, you will probably never become an expert on people, although it is highly likely that you are already an expert on behavior. You probably are thoroughly familiar with the behaviors that are appropriate for your subordinates in their specific jobs. START MANAGING THOSE BEHAVIORS.

BELIEVING THE RIGHT THINGS FOR SUCCESS

I assume that one of the reasons you are reading this book is to learn how to be more successful as a people manager, or, more specifically, how to be more successful in carrying out the face-to-face process with your subordinates. As mentioned earlier, it is quite evident to me that one of the major reasons managers are not as successful as they could be in this process is because of what they believe about their subordinates, and the people management process. As pointed out when discussing McGregor, the ways managers behave or manage their subordinates are directly related to what they believe about those subordinates. Erroneous beliefs lead managers into the self-destructive behavior of disrupting relationships, rather than helping to improve them. Stated another way, *if you believe the wrong things about your subordinates, those beliefs will be the basis for you to do the wrong things to solve problems with your subordinates.*

To put the information already covered into the proper perspective I would like to summarize for you as follows.

Point Number One

Accept that *the management function is getting things done through others.* Accept that *you need them more than they need you.* Recognize that *the rewards and punishments you get as a manager are not based on what you do, but on what your subordinates do; your subordinates are your score card. No matter what your style or skills or knowledge might be, their success or failure reflects upon you.*

If all of the above are true, then you will recognize that the only reason for being there as a manager is for you to DO EVERYTHING POSSIBLE TO HELP YOUR SUBORDINATES BE AS SUCCESSFUL AS POSSIBLE. The last thing you should do before firing someone is to look at yourself in the mirror and say "You have failed"; then tell your subordinate, "You're fired."

Point Number Two

Recognize that the management process is THINGS YOU DO, the way you behave. Your behavior is the greatest influence over your subordinates in the work environment. If you don't *do* the right things you will not be successful as a manager. There is an element of *show biz* in management. You can't influence whether it is there or not, you can choose only whether to recognize it or not. All of your behavior on the job is interpreted by your subordinates as either for them or against them. It is not enough to do what feels right, or to do what comes naturally, or to have good intentions. If you don't do the right things, you cannot expect the appropriate results. The wrong things you do are self-destructive behavior. If you don't know what to do, find out before you act. If what you are doing doesn't work, stop doing it.

Point Number Three

There is no such thing as an *amateur psychologist*, so stop trying to be one. Besides, there is no need for you to be a psychologist to be a successful manager. If you want to be a psychologist, get your Ph.D.; otherwise forget it.

Point Number Four

When you employ someone, you are not buying people, or their minds, or their values; you are only renting their behavior. As a manager, your job is not to change people, but to manage and change their behavior in your restricted environment—your lifeboat.

Point Number Five

If you want to know why people do things, forget about their motives and attitudes; you can only guess about those and you never know which of your guesses are right. Realize that people do not go through the world behaving illogically. Behavior appears illogical to them later when they discover it didn't work, or to an observer who knows a better alternative. Don't interpret the things people do in view of the alternatives you see available to them; interpret what they do in terms of the alternatives they see available to them. They don't see your alternatives, only their own. Find out what alternatives they saw, and ask why they selected the alternative they did.

If you want people to select better alternatives, let them understand the consequences of the alternative they are selecting and give them more alternatives to select from.

Point Number Six

The scientific management of man called *behavior modification* is more appropriate for you as a basis for people management, because behavior is something you are eminently qualified to deal with. You can see it when it is wrong; you can measure it; you can talk about it unemotionally; and you can see it when it changes.

6
A Practical
Approach To
Managing People
In Business

At this point, you might logically comment. "It sounds good so far, but you didn't tell me how to do it." Since the objective of this text is to present practical alternatives for you to select from when dealing with people problems, now is the time to pursue that practical approach. The first step, which is even more important than applying practical techniques to solve problems, is to analyze the problem you are faced with.

Virgil Rowland described how he gained insight into one aspect of management's problems.[1] For several years he collected responses from 8,000 managers in answer to a single question: "What areas of knowledge do you feel that you yourself need to know more about to do your own management job better, to do your direction-of-people job better?" He collected answers from first line foremen, vice presidents, and the various jobs in between, including department heads and plant managers from all kinds of companies, governmental agencies, and other organizations. After considerable analysis, he determined that all the answers fell into four categories as follows:

1. We need to know what we are supposed to do.
2. We need to know how far we are expected to go in discharging our responsibilities and authorities.
3. We need to know how well we are expected to do our jobs.
4. We need to know how well we are doing our management jobs.

[1]Virgil Rowland, *Evaluating and Improving Managerial Performance* (New York: McGraw-Hill Book Co., 1970).

The answers are disappointing, aren't they? You would think 8,000 managers of various levels would be able to describe needs much more sophisticated or exciting. Nevertheless, they are real needs. The major reason for all of the above is the lack of communication—THE LACK OF DIRECTION AND THE LACK OF FEEDBACK.

I found similar results in a survey I conducted with 4,000 managers who participated in my training programs over the last two years. I asked: "Why don't subordinates do what they are supposed to do?" These managers varied in education from high school graduates to M.D.s; they were from banking, manufacturing, retailing, utilities, and governmental organizations, and they represented every level from foreman to president, and included every function such as research, manufacturing, marketing, sales, and administration. The responses were as follows:

1. They don't know what they are supposed to do.
2. They don't know how to do it.
3. They don't know why they should.
4. There are obstacles beyond their control.
5. They don't think it will work.
6. They think their way is better.
7. Not motivated—poor attitude.
8. Personally incapable of doing it (personal limits).
9. Not enough time for them to do it.
10. They are working on wrong priority items.
11. They think they are doing it (no feedback).
12. Poor management.
13. Personal problems.

These are listed in the order they are usually given by managers. The first item on the list is given as an answer, first or second 99 percent of the time. What is surprising about this is that when managers try to solve individual nonperformance problems they *rarely* select this first answer as the place to start solving the problem. Another interesting aspect of the list is that only three items point to something inherently wrong with the worker, such as incapacity, poor attitude, or personal problems. The majority of the reasons for nonperformance are obviously there because management didn't do something right.

Most of the reasons appear to be the result of a communication problem—*lack of direction and lack of feedback*—and could be subheadings under number 12, *poor management*. If these are, in fact, the reasons subordinates don't do what they are supposed to do, it is logical that any solutions I give you in theory or practice, be directed to eliminating many, if not all, of these reasons.

WHY COMMUNICATION IS A PROBLEM

It has become quite common in recent years to blame performance problems and organizational conflicts on *poor communication*. If you review the answers above, you could conveniently generalize the overall cause for most of the reasons as poor communication. Frequently the problem is that managers and subordinates understand each other, but they are not talking about what they should be talking about. In other instances they are talking about the right things, but there is no understanding.

I remember a story in the *New York Times*, following a baseball game between the Boston Red Sox and the Yankees in Yankee Stadium. The story explained that when the score was Boston 5, Yankees 3 in the ninth inning, and the Yankees were at bat with two out and two men on base, a new relief pitcher was sent in. The coach instructed him to *pitch tough*. The first pitch resulted in a home run. Afterwards the coach was quoted by *The New York Times:* "If that's pitching tough, I don't know what pitching soft would be like." Obviously there was a communication problem.

The face-to-face medium is the predominant medium of communication between manager and subordinate, and it is of critical importance to managers. Managers harm more than help themselves in their efforts to deal with subordinates because of poor communication.

When training managers I usually ask: "What kind of problems, obstacles, or frustrations arise when you are trying to get subordinates to do something they should be doing or to stop doing something they shouldn't be doing?" They respond with high frequency that it is a communication problem, "they don't listen, they don't respond, they don't understand." Managers accuse their subordinates of failing in the communication process. A more accurate observation would be that this is the COMMUNICATOR'S FAILURE. The manager is failing in his or her communication efforts, not the subordinate. Analysis of these obvious communication failures has revealed that one of the major reasons managers are not as effective as they could be (for the purpose of influencing others) is because they are operating with the wrong definition of communication.

For example, when I ask groups of managers: "What is communication?" the usual first response is "the transmission of information." After some discussion the definition is amended to "the transmission of information between two or more parties so that it is understood." Unfortunately, this, too, is incorrect, and precisely why managers fail in their efforts to influence their subordinates.

I first learned about communication in the third grade. The teacher first described the elements of communication as similar to electrical communication. She said there must be a sender, a receiver, and a transmission. For example, in telegraphic communication between two cities, if you transmit "dot dot dash dot" from San Francisco, New York City will receive "dot dot dash dot," unless someone chops down the poles. If New York sends a signal back to San Francisco, for example, "dot dash," San Francisco will know that New York has received the message.

The teacher described how this was similar to what happens when people talk to each other. One person (the sender), through vibrations of the vocal cords, makes vibrations in the air (the transmission), and these vibrations travel through the air to the other person's ear (receiver). These vibrations activate the mechanism in the inner ear that transmits impulses through nerve synapses to the brain. Because we have learned to interpret the meaning of these impulses, we are able to understand words and, therefore, to communicate. The teacher then gave a rule as a basic guide to communication, which you are probably familiar with: "Say what you mean and mean what you say."

As a result I went through the world communicating like the wife of a once-famous television personality. On one of his television programs he explained how his wife communicated in a foreign country when she could not speak their language and they could not speak English. He said she believed that if she spoke to the natives clearly, slowly, and loud enough in English, they would understand what she was talking about, even though they did not speak English. This is not as strange as it seems; this is how many of us communicate with others, even those who speak English. Did you ever tell someone to do something and he did not do it? Wasn't your reaction to repeat it louder? You might even have said, "Did you hear what I said?" You assumed the communication failed because your dot dot dash dot was not loud enough.

But the problem is not a hearing problem. The problem is that there is no similarity between electrical or electronic communication and the communication between people. In the first place, the mind thinks at least six times faster than we can speak, and because the mind thinks so much faster, its primary function is a *reactive function*. Of course, the mind receives the information transmitted, but the information is received so fast that the mind reacts even before the message is completed. You can demonstrate this reactive principle yourself by saying to a number of people, "Say what comes to mind when I say something to you." Then say a single word to each of them, such as black, up, or hard. The responses you will most likely get will be white, down, and soft, but no one will respond with the word you said. As a matter of fact, you can say any word you choose and they will never repeat what you said. If you said to them dot dot dash dot their response might be "you are crazy."

If communication really was information transmission, and you said *white* they would say *white*; if you said *black* they would say *black*. Because the mind is primarily a reactive instrument it does not think of what you said, it thinks of something else *because of what you said*. The things you say act as triggers to create other thoughts as a reaction.

This means that if you have an idea in your head that you want to communicate to someone else, the worst thing you can do is to put that idea into the most precise and correct words you can think of and speak them. Because as soon as you say these words, the listener will hear them, *but think something else*. Because the mind is primarily a reactive instrument, successful communication is a function of THOUGHT TRANSMISSION, rather than information transmission. Therefore, if you have an idea you wish to transmit to someone else, you must say or do something that will cause that idea to appear in the other's head as a reaction to what you said or did.

For example, let's assume you and I are face to face, and my aim is to impress you with my honesty. I might begin to talk about my early childhood, my religious upbringing, and all the times I performed in an honest and trustworthy manner. As I continued relating my resistance to temptation and unrewarded honest dealings with others you might begin to wonder, "What is this guy trying to get out of me?" Voila! Thought transmission (unintended).

Let's take another example. Let's say I wanted you to be frightened, and I said to you, "Be frightened! Be frightened! Be frightened!" Obviously you will not be frightened, so I will improve my diction and say the same words even louder. Is it likely that you are going to be frightened? More likely you will be wondering what kind of a nut I am, and why I am carrying on this way. If I recognize that communication is thought transmission, however, and I want to transmit the thought *fright* to your mind, I might wait until you are relaxed, sneak up behind you, and yell as loud as I can "Boo!"; or I may approach you with a glass of water and stumble theatrically in front of you to make believe I am going to spill water all over you. In both instances you would probably jump out of your chair.

In neither instance did I say the word *fright*, but I successfully communicated the thought of *fright* to you. I did something in front of the thought called *fright* so it appeared in your head. I used thought transmission. By the same token, if I wanted the thought of my honesty to appear in your head I would be more successful if I did something in front of you that you could perceive as honest. For example, I could plant money in your path and before you get there I could come along and pick it up and ask you if it was yours. If you said *no*, I might suggest you turn it in to lost and found, or ask you to take care of it because someone may show up having lost it. You may think I'm soft in the head, but you will also think I am honest.

If you recognize that communication is thought transmission and not information transmission, you will realize that your communication efforts must be directed to doing something in front of the thoughts you want to appear in someone's head.

I know that communication as *thought transmission* is really not a new concept to you. For example, have you ever sent a gift to someone as an expression of your feelings? Did that person respond by saying, "Ah, he loves me," or "I wonder what he's up to now" (or both)? Have you ever winked at someone, or shaken your fist, or held up the middle finger, or nodded your head, or shrugged your shoulder? If you did you were using thought transmission; you acted in a way to transmit a thought; your action caused a thought to occur.

In recent years several books have appeared on the subject of something called *body language*. The writers explain in detail the message communicated by the various positions of your body. Actually, body language is an ideal example of the process of thought transmission, intended or not. What actually happens is that someone observes the position of someone else's body and because of that observation a thought appears in the head of the observer. The writings on body language are merely telling us that, regardless of your intentions, the things you do with your body are transmitting thoughts to others.

In fact, many times our facial expressions or body movements accurately transmit the thoughts we are trying to conceal with our words. For example, what thoughts are transmitted to your subordinate's head when he is talking and in the middle of his presentation you begin to read something on your desk? Intentionally or not, you have communicated, "I am bored with what's going on," or "What is on my desk is more important than what you are talking about," or "I don't really care about what you are talking about."

Information transmission as a concept interferes with managers because they waste time controlling the transmission of information and losing control over the transmission of thoughts. Managers make speeches to subordinates. They tend to do all the talking, whether it be praising, giving help, reprimanding, or trying to eliminate problems. What happens is that the manager calls in the subordinate, sits the subordinate down, and starts talking. While the boss is talking, he has no idea what thoughts are going through the subordinate's mind. The boss assumes the subordinate is thinking about what the boss is talking about, but the subordinate may be wondering how many martinis the boss had for lunch, whether the boss is in a good mood or a bad mood, or whether the boss found out about the problem they had but cleaned up and hoped the boss wouldn't discover. The simple fact of communication is that when you are talking to others, the only things you can be sure are *working* on the subject you are talking about are your brain, your mouth, and maybe their ears. If you want to know what a person's brain is working on, YOU HAVE TO MAKE SOUNDS COME OUT OF HIS MOUTH.

One manager who used thought transmission for the first time sent me this note:

This week I tried to use thought transmission as a major communication tool when working with my subordinates. Although I need a good deal more practice, and I must learn to take my time, I am thoroughly convinced of the value of this method. This is the first time I have experienced anything in management that resembles the feelings I experienced in my technical work when I solved a difficult problem or mastered a demanding procedure (the great "aha" feeling).

Instead of concentrating on different ways to say things so there will be no doubt of what is intended, I have only to think of a way to make the other person say it. The qualitative evidence of the success of this technique is overwhelming.

When I ask managers what they really want from their subordinates, they invariably answer *involvement*. When I ask them what they mean by involvement, they describe something that occurs in the subordinate's head. What they really mean is they want the subordinate's head involved in (thinking about) the subject the boss is thinking about, when the boss wants them to think about it.

The way to get this involvement and the only way to know whether or not you have it, is to MAKE SOUNDS COME OUT OF THEIR MOUTHS. The sounds that come out of their mouths had to be in their heads. This is the most fundamental way of knowing whether you are successfully transmitting thoughts, and it completely changes the emphasis of your communication techniques with subordinates. Rather than making the sounds come out of your mouth (telling people all the things you want them to know), you must do something to make the sounds come out of their mouths. That something to do is: ASK QUESTIONS.

For example, in my coaching seminars for experienced managers, my desire is to transmit the thought to the heads of the participants that 1) what they are doing is not working all the time; 2) in some instances they are doing some things that are no longer appropriate; and 3) although what they are doing may be working there may be better ways of doing it to achieve better results. The worst way for me to approach this would be for me to make a statement to them about their obvious failures in this process. If I did do that my guess would be that some of the thoughts appearing in their heads might be:

"This guy never saw me before today. How the hell does he know what kind of a manager I am?"

"You mean I'm going to have to sit here and listen to this abuse all day?"

"He doesn't know what I am doing, so how can he tell me that what I am doing is failing."

"Look at the funny shoes he is wearing."

"I wouldn't be seen dead in a tie like that."

"I wonder if we will get out of here in time to beat the traffic."

To circumvent that reaction, I use thought transmission. That is, I do something in front of those thoughts I wish to appear in their heads, and that something I do is to ask them a question, like this:

> "It appears obvious to me, looking around the room, that the majority of you managers have been managers for quite a long time; therefore, I assume you have been doing that thing called coaching or counseling or appraising or chewing for a long time. The question that occurs to me is this: 'Realizing how important time is to you managers, I wonder why you would want to take a day of your time and spend it on a subject that you obviously have been doing for many years.'" (And I shut up.)

They then tell me all the reasons why they should spend a day of time on this subject, and these answers are exactly what I would have told them, had I done it the other way. The major difference is that the sounds came out of their mouths rather than mine. And because the sounds came out of their mouths I know those thoughts were in their heads. Voila! I have been successful at transferring those thoughts from my head to their heads.

I actually did two things in this example. The first was to ask them a question and the second was to shut up. One of the primary reasons managers have difficulty communicating with subordinates is because subordinates use silence to intimidate the boss. Why is it that managers get so nervous when they ask a question and it is followed by silence? Unfortunately, because that silence seems so intolerable, managers answer their own questions. STOP DOING THAT. When you answer your own questions you are reinforcing *not answering*.

If you ask somebody a question and you really believe he is going to answer it, DON'T ANSWER IT YOURSELF. Frequently in seminars when I ask management groups a question, as above, it is followed by long periods of silence. If the participants do not respond to that question right away, I will use body language to transmit the additional thought to their heads that I do not intend to answer the question I just asked. For example, I will put down the chalk or magic marker I am holding and sit in a chair very comfortably as though I am prepared to sit there for the rest of the day. I will also SHUT UP. I will wait perhaps five minutes and if I speak again it will only be to say, "Does anybody want me to repeat the question?" I will never answer the question myself.

The fact is that silence is intimidating. I am not going to be intimidated by silence, however, I am going to use silence to intimidate the people I expect to talk to me, so they will talk to me.

Another problem with communication occurs when managers accept noncommunication. For example, how many times have you explained something to a subordinate and, after you finished, you wanted to know whether he understood it or not so you asked "Do you understand this?" The subordinate answered "Yes." The only sound you had coming out of his mouth was "yes." You do not know, in fact, whether the thing you just explained actually arrived between his ears. If you want to know whether he knows what you just explained, the only appropriate kind of question is: "Would you now explain to me what we just talked about?" or "Would you describe now how you are going to do that job based on what we just discussed?" IF YOU MAKE THE SOUNDS COME OUT OF THEIR MOUTHS THEN YOU KNOW THE THOUGHT HAD TO BE IN THEIR HEADS. If the only thing you get is a "yes," then that's all you know for sure was between their ears.

In conclusion, for you to communicate effectively for the purpose of influencing others, you must recognize that communication between people is not information transmission, but is THOUGHT TRANSMISSION. It is the process of getting a thought from your head to their heads.

Because the mind is primarily a reactive instrument, the most *ineffective* way of getting a thought from your head to their heads is to put the thought in your head in the most specific and precise words you can think of. When you do that, their minds will react to the information it has heard and, therefore, think something else.

Thought transmission is the process of saying or doing something in front of the thought you wish to appear in their heads. The only way for you to verify whether thought transmission has occurred is to make the sounds come out of their mouths, make the thoughts come out of the end of their pencils, or make them behave in a way that will occur only as a result of the thought you have transmitted (such as jumping out of a chair in response to your transmitting the thought of *fright*). This is the dilemma you are faced with:

Problem: I know I said what I want you to hear, but I'm not sure you are thinking what you heard me say.

Solution: Thought transmission.

7
Coaching For
Improved
Performance

Now we will get down to the nitty gritty of what you can do when people are not doing what they are supposed to do, or are doing something they shouldn't be doing. The process you can use is called coaching. The coaching process itself is broken down into two distinct steps:

Step 1—Analyzing the reasons why unsatisfactory performance is occurring, called coaching analysis.

Step 2—The face-to-face discussion you conduct to get the subordinate to change, called coaching.

In analyzing managers' failures in correcting subordinates' performance problems, the most frequent cause is misdirection of their corrective efforts, i.e., they concentrate on the symptoms rather than the causes of the problem. It is interesting that this phenomenon occurs only when managers are dealing with their people resources. Rarely do managers make this mistake when dealing with nonpeople resources. Wouldn't you consider it preposterous if you observed a manager who discovered an inadequacy in the lubricating system of a piece of production equipment, and he responded by having the equipment painted? Well, it appears just as preposterous to me when a manager discovers a subordinate's nonperformance, and reacts by modifying the compensation plan to create incentives for the subordinate to improve performance, when the reason for nonperformance was that the subordinate *didn't know how to do it.*

It has always appeared to me a strange contradiction that in a seminar environment, managers respond to the question, "Why don't subordinates do what they are supposed to do?" by telling me such things as "they don't know what they are supposed to do, they don't know why they should, and they don't know how to." Yet, when I discuss specific subordinate failures with individual managers they invariably state the reasons as personal, inherent, and unchangeable things in that subordinate that are beyond the control of the manager. If it appears to you that I am accusing managers of doing illogical things when dealing with individual subordinate problems, you are right. One of the major reasons managers fail to improve subordinates' performance problems is that their solutions are not related to the problems. Therefore, the logical remedy would be to develop a corrective technique to help managers identify the real causes of nonperformance. It is called *Coaching Analysis.* The purposes of coaching analysis is to identify, as specifically as possible, what the problem is and what its causes are, and to determine the appropriate corrective action.

When managers tell me they want to improve performance they are really talking about improving results; they want the outcome of performance to be better. To place coaching analysis in its proper perspective for you, let's analyze some of the elements that influence performance outcome or results. The following formula conveniently presents these varied influences.

$$A = \frac{(P + T)M}{E} = R$$

On the far right, the R represents results, those things that occur because of performance. On the far left, the A represents the abilities you expect someone to have when you hire him. This is the earliest point in the work relationship when management decisions influence the results. If you hire a 4'8" person to do a 6'3" job, there is no ladder available, you can't lower the job, and the person can't jump that high, your results will suffer. Your selection of a worker based on your evaluation of his abilities, learned and innate, will result in how closely you match the individual to the job requirements. If your selection is wrong your future results begin to be influenced at this point.

After you hire somebody and place him on the job, you expect him to do things called performance, which is represented by the P.

Performance is the *things he is paid to do* such as punching keys, pushing and pulling levers, walking, talking, sitting, standing, analyzing and solving problems, pushing brooms, or flying airplanes. His performance is the behavior you rent that is expected to produce desired results. Rarely do workers (at any level) perform the way we want them to perform as they walk in off the street. It is necessary to change and guide the quality, quantity, and appropriateness of their actions, or even just to tell them where the tools are (brooms, airplanes). This *telling* is the next most common influence we apply in business with the hopes of improving the performance. It is usually called training, and at times is called orientation; it is represented by the *T*. Sometimes it isn't called any thing because it is *rapping over cups of coffee*, and because it isn't called anything it is usually ineffective. One aspect of this training influence is that you could conceivably hire someone who has all of the abilities necessary to do the things you want them to do, but they do not *know how* to do them. If you don't train them your future result will suffer.

Another influence over performance, which, incidentally, is the one most frequently discussed by managers faced with performance problems, is motivation; this is represented by the *M*. Conceivably you could hire someone who has the abilities to do the things you require; you could place them on the job and teach them how to do it, but the results suffer because they are not motivated to do it. When managers are asked, "Why don't subordinates do what they are supposed to do?" one frequent answer is, "They don't want to do it." And when I ask them, "Why don't subordinates want to do it?" their response is, "They are not motivated to do it." Oddly enough if the first answer is, "They are not motivated," the second response usually is, "Because they don't want to." This occurs because the majority of managers today are dealing with the internalized concepts of motivation, and blame nonperformance of subordinates obviously capable of performing, on self-motivation deficiencies. When I ask them, "Why aren't your subordinates motivated?" or "Why don't they want to do what they are supposed to do?" they give such answers as:

"It's boring."

"They think it's beneath them."

"They would rather do something else."

"Peer pressure."

"They don't think they are being paid enough."

"They want to hurt the boss."

"They are not recognized for what they do."

"Fear." (They anticipate they will fail.)

These reasons for the lack of motivation do not seem so mysterious when we compare them with what we know about behavior management: *people do what they do because of the consequences of what they do.* For example, it is easy to understand why people would not do certain things if the negative consequences to them are: it is boring; they believe they would look foolish doing it; or there would be social rejection (peer pressure) if they did it. Conversely, why would someone do something if he enjoyed a positive consequence for not doing it. For example, by not doing what he were supposed to do so, he could do something else he would rather do, or if he doesn't do it someone else will do it, or he will receive attention for not performing. Therefore, as an influence over performance, motivation should be considered as the consequences to the performer for doing or not doing what you want him to do.

If your subordinates have the ability to do something and have been trained how to do it, but the consequences are not reinforcing for doing it, you can reasonably expect performance not to occur. Therefore, your future results will suffer.

Another category of major influence over performance, one that is usually overlooked by managers trying to improve performance, is the external influences, represented by *E*. External influences are those things that are obstacles to performance; things needed to support performance that fail to occur, or things that occur that should not occur and that interrupt performance. These are conditions beyond the performers' control, such as heavy snow, power failure, hurricane, fire, or theft. They can be failures of other sources to provide the required ingredients, information, or tools needed by the performer. A person could fail to do what he was supposed to do because no one provided security clearance to permit him to enter the building or area where the work must be done; or the person showed up to do it, but the co-worker did not.

Another category of obstacles, rarely recognized as the cause for failure, is the boss, who creates such things as conflicting, incomplete, or wrong instructions, or no instructions at all. I know of one company that is being strangled by its data processing system. The manager responsible for selecting the hardware knew it was not capable of handling the company's needs when he ordered it, but his boss had led him to believe the executive committee would not approve a bigger expenditure. So the subordinate *did not ask for more money;* he recommended the less expensive hardware that was inappropriate. Guess who bit the dust? It was not the boss.

As you read this, you may wonder why it is necessary to describe what must seem perfectly logical to every manager. "Why," you might wonder, "wouldn't every manager understand these influences, and, although having never written them down, follow this analysis when trying to solve performance problems?" I wonder the same thing. But I can tell you with confidence that the majority of managers in American business do not analyze their people performance problems this way. They treat a training problem with motivational efforts or an obstacle problem with training efforts. My favorite example of this occurred in a large distribution center of a retail organization that daily loaded and shipped 15 to 20 trucks of merchandise to their 600 stores.

The manager of the warehousing and shipping operation requested that I conduct a training program that would teach the truck loaders how to load the trucks properly. It seemed the trucks were arriving at the stores with heavy cases of hardware loaded on top of cartons of lamp shades, which were crushed and destroyed in the process. Cases of paint were loaded upside down and paint from the cans, which usually opened during the trip, dripped onto other merchandise, destroying it. The operations manager felt the only solution was to train the truck loaders how to load heavy items on the bottom and place cartons so the arrows on them were pointing upward. He told me that although he made speeches to the truck loaders about the cost of damage and the importance of their doing the job right, the situation was getting worse rather than better.

Before I agreed to design the training program, I told him it was necessary to observe the actual work environment. This is what I found. Each truck was forty feet long and fully enclosed. A conveyor belt extended from the warehouse past the loading dock, and into each truck. The conveyor was retracted in stages as the truck was loaded. The merchandise to be loaded on the truck was prestacked in the warehouse area approximately one hundred feet from the truck itself. When a truck was ready to be loaded, the merchandise in the warehouse was placed on the conveyor, which moved at a constant rate carrying the merchandise into the truck. Inside the truck were two truck loaders who removed the merchandise from the conveyor belt and stacked it in the truck from floor to ceiling. The conveyor ran continuously whether it carried merchandise or not. As a matter of fact one of the rules on the loading dock was: "No one turns off the conveyor except the shipping foreman."

When loading was ready to begin, the foreman made sure the truck loaders were in position inside the truck. He then signaled the people in the warehouse to load the merchandise on the conveyor. The foreman then left to inspect other trucks being loaded simultaneously. Once the merchandise began to be loaded on the conveyor in the warehouse it flowed almost continuously into the truck.

What was happening inside the truck was similar to an old "Candid Camera" episode, where a man was placed in a room with a conveyor belt coming out of a wall. He was told that pies would come out on the conveyor belt and his job was to place the pies in individual boxes. Everything went fine for a few minutes, but the speed of the conveyor was slowly increased. The man also speeded up his efforts but he couldn't keep up. It was hilarious, he was slamming pies into boxes, while other pies fell to the floor.

The situation was similar inside the truck. When a truck loader lifted a heavy case off the conveyor and was faced with placing it on top of a carton of lamp shades, the logical alternative would have been to put down the heavy carton, move the lamp shades out of the way, put the heavy case in its place and put the lamp shades on top of it. Unfortunately, if one of the truck loaders stopped to scratch his nose, a box would fall off the end of the conveyor on to the floor. In fact the loaders were not lifting boxes off the conveyor, they were catching them as they came off the end of the conveyor. If he stopped to move the box of lamp shades on the floor, he would have been buried under boxes falling off the conveyor. He could not turn off the conveyor, and there was no signal he could make to the dock foreman or the people in the warehouse loading the conveyor belt. As a result, he kept stacking boxes; hardware on top of lamp shades, arrows pointing downward or sideways; whichever way the boxes came off the conveyor, is the way he stacked them. There wasn't time for anything else.

The solution to the problem was not a training program. A shut-off switch was placed on the end of the conveyor *in the truck,* and the truck loaders were given authority to shut off the conveyor anytime it was necessary to shift cartons. After switches were installed the merchandise damaged by poor loading decreased.

The reason for poor performance seemed fairly obvious; it was the external influences beyond the control of the loaders. The manager of the operation did not correctly analyze the reason for nonperformance. If I had designed and conducted a training program the problem would not have been solved.

Each of the variables in the formula described above influence performance, hence results. All of them don't have to be bad at the same time to hurt performance. You could have a subordinate who has the ability to do a job, knows how to do it and wants to do it, but can't do it because of obstacles beyond his or her control. You could have a subordinate who does not have the ability to do what you want done, or does not know how to do it, but who wants to do it, and the unfortunate result will be the same: nonperformance and non-achievement of the end result.

It is clearly evident that an incorrect conclusion about the cause of unsatisfactory performance could lead you to apply the wrong solution. You can accurately analyze the cause of nonperformance problems by following the step-by-step process of the *Coaching Analysis.* It will lead you through a systematic, functional analysis of worker performance.

8
Coaching
Analysis

The overall purpose of the coaching analysis is to answer the question, "What is influencing unsatisfactory performance?" This is not a rhetorical question, but one posed sincerely, in contrast to the more common responses from managers after they observe a performance discrepancy, such as:

"I know what's wrong, he just needs a kick in the . . ."

"What's wrong is that we don't pay enough for the job; what else can you expect?"

"Well, you know these young kids nowadays. You can't expect much more."

"Well, you just can't get any more out of these old timers."

"We just have to get some people in here with the right kind of attitudes."

"Well, I guess it's just time for another pep talk."

"She must be having personal problems at home."

Once stated, these reasons become accepted as the real reason for unsatisfactory performance, and the *stater* acts accordingly without further analysis.

A common occupational hazard of managers is to be afflicted with the *all-seeing, all-knowing* disease. In most instances the affliction takes hold slowly and the victims don't know they have it; they just have it. Characteristic of the affliction, although it is never visible to the afflicted, is the ability to close the eyes or stare into space and know what is happening beyond the limits of one's senses. With confidence, the afflicted state they know what is going on and why things are happening, without being encumbered with mere facts. A manager ailing from this occupational disease would never ask the question, "What is influencing poor performance?" He would immediately announce that he *knows* the reasons for the performance discrepancy and exactly what to do about it.

Needless to say, this syndrome leads managers to the self-destructive behavior of aggressively applying solutions to correct nonexistent reasons for poor performance. The moral of the story is if your first response to the question, "What is influencing poor performance?" is "I know what it is," START TO WORRY.

The coaching analysis is generally done by the manager alone, if he or she has sufficient information to do it. If the manager lacks sufficient information to answer all the questions in the coaching analysis, it is necessary to collect that information either by talking to someone else who is familiar with the problem or by talking to the subordinate. If the manager talks to the subordinate for the purpose of collecting information to complete the coaching analysis, the purpose is not to discipline the subordinate or to bite him on the ankle. In other words after you observe a performance discrepancy, your first discussion with the subordinate may be to collect information about what has happened. This is separate and distinct from any discussion you might have after you have completed your analysis and identified the reason for nonperformance.

IDENTIFY THE UNSATISFACTORY PERFORMANCE

The first step in coaching analysis is to *identify the unsatisfactory performance*. This may seem like a pointless step to talk about because unsatisfactory performance has a way of jumping up and biting you. More precisely, what really jumps up and bites you is the *result* of the unsatisfactory performance.

For example, it is easy to observe from available reports that someone's sales have decreased, or someone's scrap rate has increased, or someone's error rate has increased. These observations are only results or consequences of the worker's performance. You still don't know what is causing these results. It is necessary to know what specific things a person is doing wrong, or failing to do right, to cause sales to go down, scrap rate to go up, or error rate to increase. Workers' performance is the workers' behavior, the things they do called *work*. As a manager, you must know what the inappropriate behavior is before you can select a correct solution to change it.

It seems that it would be a lot easier just to call the subordinate in and tell him to get his sales up or his scrap rate down. But have you ever done that? If you have, what was the result? Most managers tell me it works sometimes but not often enough. The reason it doesn't work is because the subordinate too frequently doesn't know *WHAT TO DO DIFFERENTLY SO THE RESULT WILL CHANGE.*

Think of the last time you did that, and let's pretend the subordinate's response to you was, "I would be glad to, boss. Please tell me what I should do differently so the result will change." Could you have told him, specifically? If you couldn't, how do you expect him to know what to do? Don't feel bad; lots of managers are saved that embarrassment because workers generally don't ask that question.

It is necessary for you to know what the subordinate is doing wrong, or failing to do right, which is giving you an unsatisfactory result. For example, are reports late because the employee doesn't start on time, wastes time on less important work, or is absent too often from his work place? Each of these is a separate worker behavior you can observe and discuss and manage. Therefore, when identifying unsatisfactory performance, keep asking yourself "*why*" until you come up with a specific behavior causing the discrepancy.

In one seminar a manager described a performance discrepancy as, "My secretary wants to mother me." He was not describing behavior, he was describing what he assumed to be an intent or a desire between his secretary's ears. When I asked him, "What does your secretary *do* because she wants to mother you," he replied with an identifiable performance discrepancy, "She gives me too much advice about my personal life." If the purpose of the coaching process is to get somebody to stop doing what he shouldn't be doing or to start doing what he should be doing, you have to identify the BEHAVIOR THAT IS THE PROBLEM.

One sales manager told me he had a long meeting with a salesman whose sales were down but, after the discussion, the sales did not go up. He asked, "What should I do now?" When I asked why the sales were down his response was, "Because he is not selling." I then asked, "What is the salesman doing wrong or failing to do right that results in what you call 'not selling'?" His answer was, "I don't know." The only logical alternative was to advise the manager to go out in the field with the salesman to observe what the salesman was doing wrong or not doing right to cause lower sales.

One of the difficulties of identifying performance discrepancies is that most managers think they do it, even though they don't. For example, if a manager is trying to correct the tardiness problem he or she will talk to the subordinate about *being late too much.* Rarely will the manager have an accurate list of the frequency of latenesses related to scheduled starting times and the specific extent of the lateness. If time cards are available, some managers might go to the trouble of extracting that information. But if time cards are not available, rarely does the manager trouble himself to keep a record. Even more important, the manager rarely knows what normal tardiness is for all the other employees.

It is quite easy for a manager, once he picks up the scent of a problem employee, to accumulate some information to support the general impression that he or she is worse than everyone else. Many years ago, when I first began teaching for the American Institute of Banking, I learned that one of the frequent reasons bank employees responsible for handling cash lost their jobs was because of the errors they made in handling cash. This is referred to in banking jargon as *differences.* Surprisingly, many banking managers complaining about errors had never identified what was the *acceptable error rate.* Although they admitted that most tellers made errors, it never occurred to them to establish an acceptable error rate.

A side effect to this kind of problem occurs when a manager is chewing on a subordinate because of a performance discrepancy and the subordinate responds with, "How come you are picking on me? Everybody does it." The boss believes the subordinate is doing a certain thing to excess. The boss also believes that thing shouldn't be done *at all, by anybody,* and he says so. The boss might say, for example, "Well, they are not supposed to be late either." The subordinate knows that everybody else does that thing occasionally and, therefore, he thinks the boss's position is unreasonable.

Let's look at it another way. Let's say you call the subordinate in because of excessive tardiness, and you tell him he must clean up the tardiness problem. Let's say you have spoken to him several times about it and it has not improved; you warn him that if he is late again you are going to have to fire him. That certainly sounds reasonable doesn't it? But do you mean that if he is late again ever in the next twenty years (if he stays in the company that long) that you will fire him? Of course, you don't mean that. Well, do you mean that if he is late once in the next two years you will fire him? Well, it is doubtful you mean that. Well then, what do you mean? If you don't really mean that, then why would you say, "If you are late again I'm going to fire you?" If there is some level of lateness that is acceptable by policy or practice, that is what must be stated as the proverbial *thin line* that people must not step over. If you will accept lateness of no more than thirty minutes and in no greater frequency than one day per month, that is what you must say. "If you are late more than thirty minutes any more frequently than one day per month, I am going to have to fire you."

Another common situation is when the boss observes a subordinate spending what appears to be too much personal time on the phone. The boss tells the subordinate, "Stop spending so much personal time on the phone." Unfortunately, the boss never identifies to the subordinate what *so much* is. Does the boss really mean no personal phone calls can be made during business hours, or does she mean if you keep it down to one personal phone call in the morning and one personal phone call in the afternoon, it's okay?

Many of the performance outcomes that are unsatisfactory in business are usually caused by the same kind of behaviors that everybody else is involved in, except this employee is doing it more than anyone else. You must identify the frequency of that undesirable behavior before you can know it is a problem and before you can start to deal with it. The best way to do that is to use a technique called work sampling. In brief, this means you actually make a record of your observations of what the worker or workers are doing at specific intervals. For example, let's assume you have concluded the reason somebody's productivity rate is down is because of excessive time away from his work station. Your impression is *Every time I walk through there Charlie doesn't seem to be around.* The next step is to conduct a work sampling.

At periodic times throughout the day, walk through the work area and observe, not only Charlie, but other workers doing similar work. Then go back to your office and make a record of what you observed for each employee. In this instance it might simply be *absence* from work station or *nonabsence* from work station. If you do this once each hour, by the end of the day you would be able to analyze the information you have collected to determine whether Charlie is actually absent more frequently than the other employees. If you cannot do it once an hour, you might do it three or four times a day, but be sure to repeat it for several days. The end result will be the same. You will have recorded observations of a group of workers permitting you to make a factual comparison of the problem employee's behavior compared to the nonproblem employees' behavior. It gives you a factual base for talking to Charlie. You can say, "Charlie, you are absent from your work station twice as much as everybody else."

The important requirement for your success is this: IF YOU ARE GOING TO DIRECT YOUR MANAGEMENT EFFORT TO MANAGING THE BEHAVIOR OF THE PEOPLE WHO WORK FOR YOU, IT IS NECESSARY FOR YOU TO KNOW WHAT THE BEHAVIOR IS NOW, SO THAT YOU ARE ABLE TO RECOGNIZE WHETHER YOUR MANAGERIAL EFFORTS ARE HELPING IT TO GET BETTER OR WORSE.

This first step is of critical importance because if you do not correctly identify the performance discrepancy, later you and the subordinate will be talking about the wrong things without eliminating the unsatisfactory performance. As mentioned earlier, your efforts to solve problems with your human resources should be just as practical and specific as your efforts to solve problems with your nonhuman resources. Have you ever taken your car in for repair and the problem was not correctly identified which resulted in replacements, adjustments, and unneeded servicing until the real problem was discovered and fixed? Well, the same waste of time and money, as well as frustration, occurs when managers don't correctly identify performance discrepancies.

IS IT WORTH YOUR TIME?

Frequently managers become aggravated over, and get involved in, so-called discipline discussions about isolated incidents that are of little importance to the job or company. Why would a manager discipline a subordinate who has been late for work once in six months, or who has submitted one sloppy report out of a hundred, or who has made any error for the first time? When I ask managers why they pounce on a single occurrence of unsatisfactory performance their usual response is, "I don't want him to get any bad habits," or "I want them to know that I know they did it," or "If you give them an inch they will take a mile."

On other occasions managers get involved in so-called disciplinary discussions with subordinates (actually, these are guidance and counseling) about things that are clearly not related to what the subordinate is being paid for. When asked why, managers say, "It might lead to bad attitudes, I have to help them maintain the right attitude." This appears to be based on the premise that managers somehow have the responsibility to guide their subordinates' total lives. I have seen workers threatened with the loss of their jobs if they didn't shave off mustaches or beards, or because their hair was too long. I have seen women whose jobs were threatened because they wore mini skirts and others because they wore slacks on the job. There was a president of a small, midwest company in the news a few years ago whose action inadvertently shut down his plant. He made a rule that employees could not smoke, even on their rest periods, because it was injurious to health.

One company president wanted me to draft a company dress code to legislate against *bralessness,* which could be used as a basis for terminating employment if violated. According to his logic, girls who did not wear bras distracted the male workers and visitors. It took quite an effort to get him to understand that he had no right (much less a method) to control what kind of underwear his employees wore. There are companies where striped or colored shirts are not an alternative to plain white; others, where a vest is mandatory; still others, where if you wear a sport jacket, you are pegged as someone who does not expect to be on the management development list. In view of managers' predominant complaint that there is not enough time to do the things they have to do, it is amazing how much time they waste, both theirs and their subordinates, on unimportant subjects and subjects unrelated to work.

The fact is that time is not available in unlimited quantities; it does require the boss's time and the subordinate's time to discuss, argue, cajole, and negotiate. If the subject is not important, why waste any time on it? If you permit yourself to become aggravated over something unimportant, not only will you be wasting your time, but you may be destroying your relationship with the subordinate. Also, termination of employment is one of the possible, realistic, and logical alternatives when you are unable to solve a problem of unsatisfactory performance. Why would you want to lose the valued performance of a subordinate over some minute aspect of performance that, in all probability, is not related to, or does not detract from, what you pay him or her to do?

That brings us to the only logical alternative for you to choose when faced with unsatisfactory performance, which is, IF IT'S NOT IMPORTANT, DON'T WASTE YOUR TIME ON IT; FORGET IT. This means that one of the first things you do after you identify a performance discrepancy is to ask yourself, "Is it worth your time?" This is not a *rhetorical question*. Just because you think it is important *does not make* it important. You must defend your decision to yourself that it is important or ignore it. I knew a sales manager in San Francisco who had a rule that if one of his salesmen did not wear a vested suit the salesman would be fired. When I asked him if he thought wearing a vest was important, his immediate response was, "Of course it is." But when I required him to describe the relevance of wearing or not wearing a vest to the achievement of the sales goal, he could not do it. He admitted he had a strong preference for the three-piece-suit image, but there was no proof that salesmen in his or any other company selling a similar product experienced unique success or failure related to wearing a vest.

An interesting corollary to this occurred when I was training a group of managers in the coaching process. After describing the above situation, I asked the managers what would their actions be in a similar situation if one of their subordinates stopped wearing a vest. One manager replied that he would fire that subordinate, and he went on to explain that his reason for doing so was that the subordinate had broken a rule established by the manager. He agreed the rule about vest wearing might be ridiculous, but, because the manager had made it, his only alternative when a subordinate broke that rule was to fire him. The rest of the class said the better alternative would be to rescind the rule. We finally convinced him that his management decisions should be functionally related to the management of his subordinates, rather than defending his mogul-emperor position by chopping off the heads of those who defy him. Why would any manager choose to waste two people's time, destroy a relationship, and/or incur turnover costs over something that *is really not important*? That would be self-destructive behavior.

So if the answer to the first question, "Is it worth your time?" is "no," the only alternative is DON'T WASTE YOUR TIME ON IT.

DO SUBORDINATES KNOW THEIR PERFORMANCE IS NOT WHAT IT SHOULD BE?

The most logical approach to determine what is influencing unsatisfactory performance should start with the most common reasons for unsatisfactory performance.

Picture yourself in a bowling alley all by yourself ready to begin a bowling game. Everything seems fine except, when you release the ball for the first time, the lights go out over the pins. You hear the pins falling but you can't see how many you knocked down. Looking around you, you see no one, so you yell out, "Hey, the lights are out over the pins and I can't see what I knocked down." A voice replies from somewhere in the area of the pins, "There are two standing." You shout, "Which two?" The voice replies, "Don't bother me. Just bowl again." Apparently there is no other alternative, so you bowl again toward the pins you cannot see. You don't hear any pins fall. After a moment the lights go on and you see the pins are set up again. So you say to yourself, "Ah, that's better," and you get ready for your second frame. As you release the ball, the lights over the pins go out again. You yell, "Hey, how about putting the lights on or tell me what is going on?" You hear the voice again say, "Please stop bothering me. I have enough to do back here. Keep bowling. I'll be back in two hours to tell you how you did."

Let's pretend you continue to bowl under those conditions. At the end of two hours the voice says, "I'm back." You say, "How did I do?" The voice replies, "Not too good." You say, "What's my score?" The voice says, "I don't know but it's terrible." Even if you were a good bowler, that would be no surprise. The reason is that you were deprived of feedback. You were not permitted to see the results of each of your actions and, therefore, you could not make effective corrections in your actions. One of the major reasons for unsatisfactory performance by workers is the lack of feedback to them about the work they are doing. It has been estimated that approximately 50 percent of the nonperformance problems in business occur because of the lack of feedback. Workers don't know how well or badly they are doing what they are doing. If a worker thinks he is doing okay, he has no reason to change what he is doing.

The most widely publicized application of feedback to improve performance in business was in the Emery Air Freight Corporation. One of the processes of this freight forwarding company was to consolidate smaller shipments from several customers into a single large container, which was then shipped as a single item by air. It was the intent of the company that 95 percent of all those items that could be so containerized would be containerized. Although there was no measurement of the actual percentage that was containerized, it was generally assumed in the organization that the 95 percent goal was being met. The managers at various levels, as well as the dock workers who actually did the work, believed they were containerizing 95 percent of those items that should be containerized. An audit of the process eventually revealed that consolidation was occurring at the 45 percent level.

The problem was corrected by providing feedback to each individual dock worker about his actual level of performance. This was accomplished with a form that required the dock worker to write the name of the shipper for each item, to note whether or not each package being processed met the requirements to be containerized, and to indicate whether or not it actually was containerized. At the end of the shift the dock worker calculated the actual percentage of those containerized against those that should have been containerized, and turned the form over to his foreman. When this form was introduced nationwide the overnight result was an increase in containerization from a national average of 45 percent to 95 percent.

Before you relegate this to the realm of magic, consider these aspects of the problem.

1. The worker knew how to do that thing called containerization.

2. The worker knew that he was supposed to do that thing called containerization.
3. All of the tools and supplies for containerization were available.
4. The worker *thought he was doing it.*

One of the reasons subordinates don't do what they are supposed to do is *because they think they are doing it.* This was clearly a feedback problem. The company was not demanding 100 percent performance; they wanted only 95 percent. The dock workers thought they were doing it at the 95-percent level, so why should they do anything different. Everytime they passed up a box they perceived it as being part of the 5 percent. Because there were no counts available to the worker he had no way of knowing whether he was passing up 5 percent, 10 percent, or 55 percent. It was a feedback problem that was fixed by providing feedback to the worker.

If workers in any job believe they are doing what they are supposed to do, why should it occur to them to do anything different? Because this is a major reason for nonperformance, the first logical step to improve performance would be to determine whether or not there is a feedback problem. Therefore in your analysis to determine "What is influencing poor performance?" ask yourself, "Does the subordinate know that performance is not what it should be?" One sure way to get the answer to that problem is TO ASK HIM. You can ask such questions as:

"Do you know what your error rate is?"

"Do you know how many days you have arrived late for work in the past six months?"

"Do you know how your error rate compares to everyone else's?"

"Do you know that you are the only one whose weekly reports are more than a day late?"

"Do you know that you frequently interrupt people when you speak at staff meetings?"

"Do you know that your subordinates are complaining that you don't permit them to express themselves?"

"Do you know that your typing produces two typing errors per page?"

"Do you know that you begin to mumble after you present your first product in your sales presentation?"

You will discover that workers frequently do not know how many errors they are making or how many days they actually come to work late. At times a worker will know how many errors he is making, but will assume everyone else is making the same number of errors. In other words, each knows his own level of performance, but thinks everyone else's performance is just as bad.

Sometimes workers know they are doing things they should not be doing, BUT THEY DON'T KNOW IT IS A PROBLEM. The feedback you give them is to let them know that what they are doing is not satisfactory. The first step to solve a tardiness problem is to tell the worker how many times he has been tardy, that you don't accept it, and ask him to correct it, as follows:

> You: Charlie, I notice that for the last week you have been late for work three out of the five days. This is not acceptable performance; would you please come to work on time?
>
> Charlie: Okay, I sure will try.
>
> You: Thank you.

That is called a feedback discussion. Notice that your statement also referred to expected performance: "Would you please come to work on time?"

You will eliminate some performance problems by giving feedback to the worker on a one-time basis. If you have identified a problem behavior, such as *excessive time away from his work station*, the first conversation with your subordinate should be a feedback statement such as, "Tondalayo, I notice you have been away from your work station more than six times each day this week. Would you please restrict your absence to the scheduled rest periods?"

If a worker's productivity is unsatisfactory because he doesn't know how he is doing, he may need feedback on an hour-to-hour basis. You can, in fact, increase productivity in certain jobs by providing feedback about individual productivity hourly. I am not recommending that you spend all your time telling workers how they are doing each hour. This requires the creation of a feedback system that operates between the worker and the work so the feedback does not pass through the boss to get to the worker, and does not depend on the boss for the worker to get it. This can be simple actions of checking or counting or comparing by the worker at established intervals of the work process, according to time or phase completion. If a bowler keeps his own bowling score he is operating his own feedback system.

One interesting aspect of feedback occurred with the vice president of a division of a large corporation. He told me about one of his subordinates who was responsible for preparing some comprehensive marketing reports involving market analysis of specific projects. The vice president complained that these reports, when submitted, were invariably incomplete, because they didn't answer all the questions the vice president thought should be answered. At my suggestion that the subordinate might not know what finished was supposed to look like, the vice president and the subordinate together worked up a list of key questions that should be answered in all reports.

The vice president contacted me shortly afterward to tell me he did that but that the next report also had been incomplete. I asked the vice president whether or not the subordinate was checking that list of questions against the completed report before the report was forwarded to the vice president. The vice president said he didn't know but would find out. He got back to me shortly afterwards, and told me that, amazingly enough, although the subordinate had the list of questions, he was not checking the list against the completed report before submitting it to the boss. The vice president instructed the subordinate to check all future reports against the list before submitting the report. Subsequently all reports submitted were satisfactory.

In this instance the first thing the vice president did to correct the problem was to establish a *basis* for feedback for the subordinate (what finished was supposed to look like). This provided an ideal basis for the subordinate to give feedback to himself after completing the report, to determine whether or not the report was finished.

In summary, performance problems caused by lack of feedback can only be solved by providing feedback to the worker. It seems logical and easier to do that with routine or highly repetitive jobs, but it is also critically important in the so-called creative or unmeasurable jobs. If you don't know how to measure the performance of a certain job, it doesn't mean the job can't be measured; it just means you don't know how to measure it.

If the answer to the question: DO SUBORDINATES KNOW THEIR PERFORMANCE IS UNSATISFACTORY? is *no*, the only solution is LET THEM KNOW.

DO SUBORDINATES KNOW WHAT IS SUPPOSED TO BE DONE?

As you recall, one of the most prevalent responses managers give to the question, "Why don't subordinates do what they are supposed to do?" was "They don't know what they are supposed to do." Part of not knowing *what is supposed to be done*, is not knowing *when* it is supposed to be done. Frequently subordinates don't complete a job or project on time because they didn't know when it was supposed to be finished so they didn't start on time. An even more critical part of this problem is, *What is it supposed to look like when it is finished?*

Has a subordinate ever done a job for you that turned out to be less than what you expected, and when you described how much more work had to be completed, his response was, "Oh, I didn't know that's what you wanted. I'll be glad to do that." If so, the problem was *they didn't know what finished was supposed to look like.* Too frequently, especially in creative areas, subordinates are given jobs to do but the only one who can recognize when it is finished is the boss. The result is that subordinates keep bringing what they believe to be completed projects to the boss and are repeatedly told, "No, that's not what I wanted." I am not talking about those ridiculous situations where the boss clearly identifies to the subordinate what finished should look like, but when the completed project is submitted the boss *decides* something else should be done rather than what was previously agreed to.

Here is one manager's description of how he discovered unsatisfactory performance was occurring because the subordinate didn't know what was supposed to be done. His subordinate was a sales administrator with about one year's experience. His major complaint about her was that when she worked on specific assignments she did not analyze situations in depth to reach solutions or suggest alternative solutions. When she presented an incomplete job to him, his usual response was to accept it and complete it himself without explaining what else he wanted and why. He justified his actions by telling himself he had hired the wrong person for the job, that she was incapable of handling it. Before firing her, he decided to try coaching analysis as an alternative.

"Mary, on the recent market price analysis you prepared for me, were you satisfied with the finished product?" Her response was, "Yes, I gave you what you asked for." I then showed Mary the form she had completed and asked her if there was any additional information she could have included that would have helped me reach a decision as to the price we should charge for our product. I had already taken my analysis from the file folder so the additional information I had included, which she should have done, could not be seen.

After some thought she suggested we could add the strength relationship of our product versus the competitive product. I told her that was a good idea, and asked if there was anything else.

"Not really," she said, "all I can think of now is to plug in a price for our product based on the amount of gross profit we think is necessary." I continued with, "Can we sell a product in the market at a higher price than competition?" She agreed that we could not, and said that if we are looking at a product where the strengths of our product and the competition's product are equal, we could only plug in the same price of the competitive product on the form and then compare our cost figure, and list the gross profit in the appropriate place. She was correct.

The analysis was now complete and ready for review and approval by top management. Knowing that pricing is not always that easy, however, I asked Mary how we could arrive at a price if the strengths of the two products were not equal or if other running properties were different. SHE DID NOT KNOW. I then showed her step-by-step how to figure it out, if we knew what the competitor's prices were and what prices we would have to charge to be at parity. I was surprised to see that she even wrote down the step-by-step procedure. I further explained that if our product had superior running properties how much premium we could, in reality, expect to receive, and, on the other hand, if our product was inferior in some way, how we must reduce our prices by a certain factor. I told Mary that when I asked for a market price analysis I expected a complete job just as we had reviewed. She told me she would include the foregoing information in the future. She also said that no one, including me, had ever taken the time to show her how to compare two products with each other. She further stated that when I had asked her to prepare market price analysis I had not mentioned that its purpose was to be able to establish a price for our product.

Future price analytical work I have asked her to do has been produced as I requested. I discovered that IF SHE DIDN'T KNOW WHAT I WANTED SHE COULD NOT SUPPLY WHAT I WANTED.

Another manager, of an electrical engineering testing laboratory, was complaining to me about a subordinate who always "went too far" in collecting unnecessary data in a testing project. I asked the manager how the technician could know when he had gone far enough in collecting data. The manager's response was, "If he will come to us we will tell him as he progresses with each project." Invariably the subordinate was advised by his manager that he had not gone far enough or he had gone too far in collecting data. Here was a situation where the only one able to recognize what finished looked like was the manager. This manager eventually agreed (reluctantly) that the best solution was to give sufficient information to the technician so *the technician* could recognize finished when he saw it.

Certainly if you just told a subordinate what is supposed to be done, you feel safe in assuming he or she now knows what to do. Your confidence in your assumption would be directly related to how specific and complete you were in describing what *was supposed to be done*. (Unfortunately the sounds came out of your mouth not his or hers). As you and your instructions to subordinates get separated by distance, as well as by other managers who must pass on your instructions, you should have less confidence in knowing that subordinates know what is supposed to be done.

For example, if your company is like most companies, you probably use experienced employees to orient new employees to the job. When you do this do you give a check list to the experienced employee to follow as a guide in the orientation, to insure that all the critical information relative to the job is covered? Do you ask the experienced employee to annotate the check list to indicate that all items needed to be covered were covered, and that the new employee understands what must be done? At the completion of the orientation do you quiz (formally or informally) the new employee to find out for sure he knows what is supposed to be done? If your company is like most companies, you probably don't do any of that. So why are you surprised six months later, when the new employee does not do something he is supposed to do, and when you face him with it his response is, "I didn't know I was supposed to do that"? Of course, you can feel better if you say such things as, "Don't give me that excuse, you had orientation just like everyone else," or "You have been around here long enough, you should know better." But the real problem is HE DIDN'T KNOW WHAT WAS SUPPOSED TO BE DONE. In situations like this, managers usually treat the subordinate's comments as empty excuses rather than feedback to the manager that the management process is failing, and the employees should be informed about what is supposed to be done. If you don't organize the orientation process there will be some things left out.

Let's look at another nuance of this problem of *not knowing*. Let's assume you have to leave your office in a hurry for some reason, but you have a report you want done by subordinate A. Subordinate A is not available, so you speak to a peer manager and ask them to tell subordinate A to do the report for you. When you return to work you discover subordinate A has not done the report. Perhaps there have been other occasions when subordinate A has not done certain things that were supposed to be done, and you consider this incident *the . straw that broke the camel's back*. So you call in subordinate A to chew him out. The conversation might go something like this:

> Boss: Subordinate A, I have been watching your performance over a period of time now, and it has come to my attention that there are instances where your performance has not been satisfactory. I don't know whether this is caused by inability on your part, or by some latent resistance to authority that results in your disregarding certain tasks and deadlines that are important to the rest of the organization, whether or not they are important to you. Now I have not brought this to your attention earlier because I was waiting

        to see whether a pattern was developing. This last incident certainly brings me to that conclusion. What do you have to say for yourself?

Sub. A: What last incident?

  Boss: Your failure to have that report ready for me today.

Sub. A: What report?

  Boss: The report you were supposed to do yesterday afternoon.

Sub. A: I don't know of any report I was supposed to do yesterday afternoon.

  Boss: Mr. Peer told you yesterday afternoon that I wanted such and such a report prepared by today.

Sub. A: I didn't see Mr. Peer at all yesterday.

  Boss: You mean Mr. Peer didn't ask you to do such and such a report for today.

Sub. A: No.

Oops! You just discovered that nonperformance occurred because he didn't know what he was supposed to do. What usually happens next is the boss continues on the subject of unsatisfactory performance just as though the *last straw* had really happened. Rarely does the boss apologize and suggest they both forget the whole thing.

If you had been using coaching analysis regarding this incident of nonperformance, you would have asked Mr. Peer if he had passed on your message yesterday. If the answer was *no*, you could correct the performance discrepancy problem by going to subordinate A and requesting that the report be done. You could have spoken to subordinate A first, but your first question would have been to find out if yesterday's message was received. If subordinate A had said "no," you would have discovered that unsatisfactory performance was caused by not knowing what was supposed to be done. The action to correct it would be to *ask subordinate A to do the report*.

When you discover the reason for nonperformance is *they don't know what they are supposed to do*, the solution is LET HIM OR HER KNOW WHAT IS SUPPOSED TO BE DONE, AND WHEN.

This cause of nonperformance is not a skill deficiency. In these situations subordinates know how to do something, but they just don't know when it should be started, or when it should be finished, or what finished is supposed to look like (how good it is supposed to be).

Therefore, the second logical step in your analysis of performance problems is to look for a most common reason for nonperformance, by answering the question, DO SUBORDINATES KNOW WHAT IS SUPPOSED TO BE DONE, AND WHEN? If the answer is *no*, TELL THEM and the problem will go away.

ARE THERE OBSTACLES BEYOND THEIR CONTROL?

You will recall that one of the variables in our formula depicting the major influences affecting results was E, the external influences beyond the control of the performer. Therefore, in your coaching analysis to determine what is influencing poor performance, the next logical step is to determine whether or not there are obstacles beyond the subordinate's control. It is important that you pursue this question early for several reasons. First of all, it is highly likely you will discover performance interference by obstacles without even talking to the subordinate. This puts you in a position to remove those obstacles, permitting the performance discrepancy to disappear without even consulting the subordinate. Secondly, if the subordinate's performance is being adversely affected by obstacles beyond his control, it is really your problem, not the subordinate's problem. Frequently these obstacles include interference by higher level managers, as well as others who fail in their service and affect your subordinate's performance adversely. As the boss, you may have to use your knowledge, experience, and influence to modify or remove those obstacles to solve the problem. Thirdly, if it is not the subordinate's behavior that is affecting the consequence, why talk to the subordinate?

Examples of obstacles beyond the subordinate's control could be such things as nondelivery of raw materials, unfinished prework, late or incorrect reports or data, equipment failure, conflicting instructions, all of which the subordinate requires to perform. Picture a subordinate scheduled to come in on Saturday to run a special program on the computer only to find the building's electrical system not working because the elevator system is being repaired. The result is nonperformance. There are other obstacles, such as thirty-six inches of snow, floods, hurricanes, accidents, illness, and death (of others). You may not be able to eliminate some of these obstacles, but you may be able to help lessen their effect on performance.

Besides observation, the most direct source of collecting information to determine whether or not there are obstacles beyond a subordinate's control is to discuss the performance problem with the subordinate. Subordinates are not reticent to point out the many obstacles that interfere with their performance. Unfortunately, many managers make up their mind in advance that the reason for nonperformance is caused by poor attitude, lack of self-motivation, or stupidity; therefore, any comments about obstacles are written off as excuses. This MAGIC that managers perform, is to judge whether a subordinate's comments are valid reasons or excuses without investigating to collect additional facts.

I know it is frustrating to be in high gear chewing out a subordinate only to be presented with factual information about obstacles to performance you were unaware of. When it happens to you, you feel like an idiot. You can become a bigger idiot by waving it away as unimportant, or you can swallow your pride, apologize, and go away to investigate. There is another alternative, of course, and that is not to get into a chewing session until you find out who is to blame for what. If there really are obstacles beyond the subordinate's control, then your concern is not about the subordinate's behavior, but about the obstacles. The solution to that problem is REMOVE THE OBSTACLES.

When trying to answer the question, "Are there obstacles beyond the subordinate's control?" it is your responsibility to collect enough information to determine whether or not the obstacles the subordinate talks about are real or imagined. If the obstacles are real, it is also your responsibility to do what is necessary to remove them or circumvent their influence. In your quest to answer the question, "What is influencing unsatisfactory performance?" you should answer the question: ARE THERE OBSTACLES BEYOND THEIR CONTROL? If the answer is *yes*, REMOVE THEM and performance will become satisfactory.

DO SUBORDINATES KNOW HOW TO DO IT?

You will recall that the second most prevalent response to the question, "Why don't subordinates do what they are supposed to do?" was "They don't know how to do it." This is a common reason for nonperformance primarily because of the assumptions we make that learning has taken place. It is sad but true that those responsible for training in business have not universally accepted the binding axiom for all trainers, *If the student hasn't learned, the teacher hasn't taught.* As a result, there are lots of activities going on that are *called* training, but there is very little *learning* taking place. Approximately 80 percent of those people I contact in business responsible for creating or conducting training programs have never been taught how to teach. They are designing and conducting programs that concentrate on teaching rather than learning. They concentrate on what is taking place with the instructor, rather than concentrating on what should be taking place with the student. The most telling clue to identify teachers who don't know how to teach is their comments about the students, such as "Boy, that was a dead group," or "They sure were unresponsive," or "That group was not too sharp."

Another remarkable failing trait that formal business training programs share is *the lack of testing.* At the graduate and under-graduate levels, testing is used as another step in the learning process to provide opportunities for students to apply what they have learned, as well as for them and the teacher to receive feedback indicating whether learning has in fact occurred.

Recently a conversation with the director of training of one large corporation went something like this.

> Me: Do you use testing to determine whether or not your training is achieving learning objectives?
>
> Trainer: Yes, we do.
>
> Me: How do you do it?
>
> Trainer: We don't use paper and pencil tests; actually each trainer makes those observations.
>
> Me: How do they do that?
>
> Trainer: They gauge the responses of the participants throughout the training session and at the end of the session.
>
> Me: Do the instructors have a check list, or something specific they can use to help them identify those responses that would indicate whether or not learning has occurred?
>
> Trainer: No. Because of the trainers' long experience in these areas, they have a feel for this.

Me: Well then, do they apply some kind of specific measurement to determine the levels of learning in each individual?

Trainer: No, they just get a general feel for how each individual is doing.

Me: But if you don't have a check list or a guide to specify the learning that is expected to take place, how does the instructor recognize it when he sees it?

Trainer: The things we have to teach are quite complicated and cannot be measured quantitatively. We rely a great deal on the experience and knowledge of the trainers; after all, their experience has to be worth something.

Subsequently I had the opportunity to view one of the trainers in action; he talked and the students listened; they were not required to respond in any way. At the end of a two-hour session only one student had taken notes and only two asked any questions, and the students were not required to demonstrate learning. Not only was there no testing, verbal or otherwise, to determine whether learning had occurred, there was no teaching.

Another cause of nonlearning in business is that common practice of assigning experienced employees to train new employees. The question is, "Who taught the experienced employees how to teach?" The answer is invariably *no one*. Experienced employees are usually selected as the trainers because they do their jobs better than most. Unfortunately, the moment they are asked to show (teach) the new employees how to do it, they are being given a new job as teachers, which they don't know how to do. If there is no teaching happening how can you expect learning to happen? Just because two people spend a certain amount of time sitting or standing close to each other, looking at and talking about the same things, does not mean that teaching or learning is happening. Because a manager has once said, "Let there be training," his reaction to a new employee's performance discrepancy in the future will not include the possibility that "they don't know how to do it." It will be assumed that because the new employee was exposed to the training, the learning occurred.

In my five-day seminar, "Training for Trainers," there is resistance on the first day because experienced trainers can't understand why they should be there. But on the last day they express their amazement at how much they learned about something they thought they had been doing well for five to fifteen years.

One manufacturing supervisor wanted to know what to do about those employees that obviously "don't give a damn." When I asked him to give me an example he described a situation where a new employee had been trained by an experienced employee on a custom-designed automatic manufacturing machine. When the training period was over the new worker was assigned to operate his own machine. Almost immediately he did something wrong, which caused $15,000 damage to the machine. The supervisor explained that the expensive damage to the machine was obviously the result of the worker's "I-don't-give-a-damn" attitude. The rest of our conversation went like this:

Me: This doesn't appear to be a problem of attitude. It appears that you made a bad $15,000 decision.

Supv.: What do you mean by that?

Me: Did you know that a mistake in operating the machine could cause $15,000 worth of damage?

Supv.: Yes.

Me: Then what facts did you have to lead you to believe that the new worker would not damage the machine?

Supv.: He was trained in how to operate it.

Me: You told me that he went through something called training, but how did you know at the end of the training that he knew how to operate the machine?

Supv.: Look, you have to assume some things in the world; if a man is trained in how to do something I have to assume he knows how to do it.

Me: Who was the trainer?

Supv.: Our most experienced machine operator.

Me: Was he ever taught how to teach?

Supv.: No.

Me: Did he have a written outline to follow in carrying out the training program?

Supv.: No.

Me: At the end of the training did the trainer give you a list of those critical aspects of machine operation that must be covered in training and indicate that they were covered and understood by the worker?

Supv.: No.

Me: Then how do you know the new worker knew how to operate the machine after the so-called training was finished?

Supv.: What do you want me to do, train every new employee myself? I just don't have enough time for that. That production floor is like a mad house.

Me: No, it wouldn't be logical to expect you to carry out the training. But why wouldn't you conduct some kind of test at the end of the training to find out whether learning has actually occurred.

Supv.: Look, I'm not a college professor. I'm a production supervisor trying to produce the product as economically as possible. I just don't have time for all that stuff.

Me: Let's look at this another way. How much justification does your company require if you want to spend $15,000?

Supv.: Well, they would want quite a bit of justification. If it's a purchase they would want at least three estimates, and they usually want to know why it can't be done without the expenditure in the first place.

Me: That sounds typical, and rightly so. But it appears that you didn't go through any justification to spend the $15,000 on the machine that your subordinate damaged.

Supv.: Wait a minute. I didn't damage the machine. It was the worker who made the decision to screw it up, not me.

Me: It appears that way, but these are the facts: 1) you knew that the machine could be damaged to the tune of $15,000 if it were operated improperly; 2) you assigned the worker to the machine without having any facts to indicate that the worker *would not damage the machine.*

Supv.: Wait a minute. I didn't assume the worker would damage the machine.

Me: Right. But you did assume that the worker would not damage the machine. When you assigned that worker to that machine, you were actually stating, "I, the supervisor, sound of mind and body, am making the decision to assign the new worker to operate this expensive machine, which could be damaged to the tune of $15,000. I have justified this decision by gathering enough facts to lead me to believe that the worker will not do those inappropriate things to damage the machine." You, in fact, made that $15,000 decision without any justification whatsoever. You merely assumed the worker knew how to operate the machine because he was exposed to something called training.

Supv.: I understand what you are saying. When I assign somebody to do something, that decision is worth the value of the highest cost to the company if that worker screws up. But I am not capable, nor do I have the time, to sit down and design training programs and high class tests.

Me: You are certainly right, and it wouldn't be reasonable to expect you to design a training program. Nevertheless, if you are aware of the combination of those critical conditions and worker actions that lead to destructive results, then it would be fairly simple at the end of training for you to ask a list of questions that would face the workers with those critical conditions to determine whether or not they select the appropriate alternative action (and, therefore, prevent the destruction from occurring).

The problem is that because you see training taking place, you assume that learning is taking place; because you assume learning has taken place, you have to find another reason for the screw-up when it occurs, such as, "They don't give a damn."

Let's consider another question. If a student attending a five-day training program in your organization does not attend for one of the five days, is the student scheduled for a sixth day to make up for the day missed, or does the instructor spend twenty minutes with the student on the following day to make up for the lost time? If your company is like most companies, the instructor will spend the twenty minutes with the student to make up for the lost time. You might ask yourself, "Then why isn't the training program four days and twenty minutes instead of five days?" How can a student make up for a day's training in twenty minutes? Because the worker's record indicates he or she attended the training program, the manager assumes learning has occurred.

Another aspect of the learning problem relates to that big difference between knowing what should be done and having the opportunity to do it. For example, reading how to fly an airplane is quite different from flying a real airplane. Reading how to bowl is quite different from doing it. Reading how a skill should be carried out is entirely different from the actual practice of using that skill. A significant amount of training in business is not successful because it exposes employees to knowledge about how a skill should be performed, but does not provide them with the opportunity to apply that skill until the real job must be done. They don't get a chance to practice. You may be faced with a performance discrepancy of a subordinate who possesses all the innate qualities necessary to perform, who may have a high desire to perform, and there are no obstacles beyond his control to prevent him from performing, but nonperformance is occurring because HE DOESN'T KNOW HOW TO DO IT. It could be he did it so long ago he has forgotten how to do it, or it could be he learned what he *should do*, but was never provided the opportunity of *doing it*.

It serves no practical purpose for you as a manager to make such observations as, "I can't believe that anyone who has been around here as long as you have does not know how to do that," or "If you have been to the training like everybody else you should be able to do it," or "You should have learned that by now." When training is supposed to take place, test to determine whether learning has occurred, and you will not make wrong assumptions. In your quest to answer the question, "What is influencing unsatisfactory performance?" one key question you should answer is, DO THEY KNOW HOW TO DO IT. If your nonperformance problem is occurring because "The subordinate doesn't know how to do it," the solution is PROVIDE TRAINING OR PRACTICE.

DOES NEGATIVE CONSEQUENCE FOLLOW PERFORMANCE?

You will recall that the science of behavior management is based on the premise, *all behavior is a function of its consequences*. The scientific practice of behavior modification has demonstrated that behavior followed by a positive consequence will increase in frequency; behavior followed by a negative consequence will decrease in frequency. Your understanding of this contingent relationship between behavior and consequences provides you with new alternatives in answering the question, "What is influencing poor performance?" For example, it would be perfectly logical for you to explore the possibility that desired performance is not occurring because a negative consequence or a painful event is experienced by the performer following the desired performance. As mentioned earlier, it frequently happens in business that workers who do the nasty tasks well, get to do all the nasty tasks.

One of my early work experiences while in high school was for a large furniture store as a part time lamp assembler, paid by the hour. One of the consequences of getting my work done quickly was to go home early. Now going home early from work could be construed as a positive consequence under certain conditions, but not if you needed the money and I did. As you might guess, my speed on the job was quickly replaced by thoroughness; a thoroughness, I might add, that was far in excess of what was expected. The consequence was that I rarely went home early.

About two months after I started the job, the manager told me they occasionally needed someone to help with furniture deliveries and, if I wanted to, I could go out on the delivery truck after my lamp assemblies for that day were finished. Now it might appear miraculous to some, but it so happened that my accumulation of two months lamp-assembling experience had the sudden effect of improving my speed, so that all the assigned lamp-assembling work was completed in about half the previous time. The consequence was that I was available to help on truck deliveries every day they needed me. Incidentally, the work on the truck turned out to be just as great as I thought it would be.

Recently a manager who supervises five secretaries, who work for eight executives, described a situation where performance was being followed by negative consequences to the performer. He said the rule was that when any secretary finished her work she was supposed to contact the secretary with the most work and take on part of that work herself. But in practice it was not occurring. Each secretary was apparently stretching her own work to avoid finishing. This is a frequent occurrence where the only consequence to those workers who work fastest, is to get more of somebody else's work.

In an ice cream company one job the workers considered most undesirable was on the popsicle machine. The operator had to bag the popsicles being made and place them in a carton. The job was undesirable because of the speed at which the machine produced popscicles, and because the worker had to stand and work alone. Because the popsicle machine was considered such a "bad job," the workers were rotated through that job one day at a time. The manager complained that most of the workers did not do this job very well; the popsicles would pile up and fall on the floor and frequently the machine would have to be stopped so the worker could catch up. To his surprise, even the workers who did well on that job at first couldn't seem to do it later on. Although the workers were rotated, those who did this job best tended to be rotated through that job more frequently than the rest of the workers. There was an obvious negative consequence to good performance.

As another example, a manager was having difficulty getting members of his staff to recommend programs that would contribute to the organization's overall effectiveness. He complained about their lack of creativity, initiative, and interest in contributing to the organization. But in his staff meetings where these suggestions came forth, his response to an idea was to imply that it was impractical or unbusinesslike. If an idea was accepted his usual response was, "That's a good idea; because it's your idea why don't you follow through on it." The consequence of coming up with ideas was to be embarrassed or to end up with more work.

In labor intensive production situations, supervisors frequently talk about new workers who *start off with a bang,* showing potential as future high producers, but who seem to *fizzle out* and their production gets just like the rest. In some work situations one of the consequences of producing more than your fellow workers is to drink your coffee alone or to lose your teeth in the parking lot. Rate busters are not very popular people.

One common complaint of executives in smaller organizations is, *people in this organization don't think for themselves or do anything on their own; they look for the bosses' okay on everything before they do it.* You might wonder whether anyone ever does anything on his own in those organizations. The answer is yes, once in a while. But when someone does do something on his own and if it works, the best thing that can happen is for the boss to tell him eleven other ways it could have been done better. If the independent action didn't work out, the consequence varies from being ridiculed by the boss in front of others to being ostracized by the boss for several days or being permanently damaged by the label of *screw-up.*

Incidentally managers are unaware that, in their dealings with subordinates, they fall victim to *thought transmission* and thereby unknowingly dispense negative consequences intended as gems of wisdom. One thing that happens when a subordinate presents an idea to the boss is that the boss frequently thinks of another idea. Because the mind is a reactive instrument, the presentation of the subordinate's idea created a thought reaction in the boss's head, which caused that other idea to appear.

Quite naturally because the boss's idea was triggered by the subordinate's idea the boss's idea will probably be a better one. If you combine this with another occupational disease of management which is *the boss thinks the boss's ideas are always the best* (even if they are not) you create a situation where there is only negative consequences to a subordinate, who presents ideas to the boss. The boss always comes up with another idea, and it has to be done the boss's way. As a manager you can't stop thought transmission from occurring when your subordinate presents ideas to you, but you can prevent it from being a negative consequence by using thought transmission to make your new idea come out of his mouth.

There are situations in the work world where the obvious negative consequence to performance is failure on the part of the performer. These failures frequently occur because the performer does not know how to perform correctly. When workers are required to do things they don't know how to do or are incapable of doing, they usually fail; this is a negative consequence to them. Frequently sales people do not try to sell one or more of their company's products because 1) they know the product does not perform the way it should, 2) the product will invariably not be delivered on time, or 3) the salesman is not technically conversant with that product and, therefore, will not be able to answer a real customer's questions. The result of the first two is the customer will be aggravated and will vent that aggravation all over the salesperson. The third reason results in an embarrassment and most frequently a lost sale. Who wants to lose sales?

A salesman with a company that introduces five to fifteen new products a year was recently explaining that he was in danger of losing his job. He was in trouble because he rarely sold any of the new products until ten to twelve months after they were introduced. This is the reason he gave:

> "When this company introduces new products, the situation is always screwed up. One time they come out with the literature, but there is no product available; the next time they come out with the product, but there is no literature available. Another time they will release a new product, but then someone in Engineering decides to modify the tool used to apply it, which results in the new product being available but the tools needed to apply it are on back order."

> "I used to sell these new products, but I felt like an idiot in front of the customer when I couldn't explain why the new products I just sold him couldn't be delivered."

There are certain jobs with exposure to customers or the public, wherein the worker is subjected to above-average verbal abuse, which may include four letter expletives. Under these conditions the consequences of talking to customers is to suffer. Occasionally new workers entering these positions perform poorly, by overreacting argumentively, just as though the complaints were directed at them personally, rather than at the company or the product. Perhaps the worker sheds tears, absents himself from the work station, arrives late for work, or doesn't come to work at all. It is easy for us to accuse them of making mountains out of mole hills and label them as emotionally unstable for that job. Nevertheless, a vital part of the training of workers in high volume, customer service jobs is to teach the worker how not to react personally to the customer's comments. By teaching the worker how to behave appropriately, you are eliminating a skill deficiency, which has the effect of eliminating the negative consequences.

On rare occasions you will be faced with situations when nonperformance will occur because a worker will persistently overreact to what is customarily accepted by the rest of us as normal pain in that job. If you cannot remove the pain (negative consequence) or lessen it through training, remove the worker from the job.

As an example, a young woman employed with a retail company for about five years was suddenly on the verge of losing her job because of high absenteeism. Her manager thought her absences were due either to "female problems" or personal problems, neither of which she chose to discuss. He was resigned to losing the employee because he had to take a hard stand on absenteeism.

When I interviewed the employee it was revealed that her absenteeism began only after she was transferred from the merchandise labeling department to the garment labeling department. Both jobs paid the same. The only difference was that in the merchandise labeling department the labels were put on merchandise with an adhesive, whereas in the garment labeling department the labels were put on the garments by using a pinning machine. The pinning machine was like a hand held gun that actually shot straight pins through the label and the material. It was quite common for new workers to occasionally shoot a pin into their fingers, along with the label and the garment. The injury was painful when it occurred, but never serious, and it rarely happened to experienced pinning machine operators.

The worker in question had never had a pinning accident, but she expressed a strong fear of one happening. She related that when a job opened up in the merchandise labeling department she had asked the supervisor to transfer her back again, but he had refused. When the supervisor was asked why he would not transfer her back to the other department, he said, "Of course she told me she didn't like the pinning machine, but she was blowing it out of proportion; I showed her the right way to do it; she's just going to have to grow up and learn how to do this job. I told her I would transfer her to the merchandise department when she learned how to do the pinning job and stopped being so childish about it." (Sounds like the dark ages, doesn't it?)

The action taken was to transfer the girl immediately to the merchandise labeling department. The miraculous result was that the absenteeism problem disappeared. The moral of the story is that the manager could have solved his own problem (the worker absenteeism) had he accepted the employee's view of the negative consequences of performance.

These are all examples of negative consequences happening to workers when they perform the desired task. Managers usually search for a lack of a reward (positive consequence) as a reason for non-performance, but rarely does it occur to them that unsatisfactory performance is occurring because the worker is punished when the job is done right. If logic would lead managers to believe that *workers do not do things they are not rewarded for,* why wouldn't the same logic lead managers to believe that *workers do not do things they are punished for?*

The obvious solution to this kind of problem is to remove the negative consequences. But you may say, "Every job has negative consequences; after all work is not play; and suppose you can't remove the negative consequences." Of course, you are right. But you will have to admit that *all play requires work and includes some negative consequences.*

The most popular participative sports today require physical exertion, cause blisters and minor injuries, as well as social embarrassment far greater than what might be experienced on the average job. So why are these sports so popular? Is it because we love punishment? The reason is that these sports also provide positive consequences that compensate for, or outweigh, the negative consequences. It is logical to remove negative consequences that are causing nonperformance, but if the negative consequences cannot be removed, the solution is to provide positive consequences where there are none, to counterbalance the negative consequences.

If you recognize the scientific fact that *behavior is a function of its consequences* you will expand your analysis of reasons for unsatisfactory performance and will be able to solve more performance problems. In your search to discover what is influencing poor performance, answer the more specific question: "Does a negative consequence follow performance?" If the answer is yes, the solution is CHANGE THE CONSEQUENCE OR TRANSFER THE INDIVIDUAL, as follows:

1) change the consequences by eliminating the negative consequence
2) change the consequences by providing an immediate positive consequence for the same performance to outweigh the negative consequence.

DOES POSITIVE CONSEQUENCE FOLLOW NONPERFORMANCE?

Because the scientific study of behavior modification has demonstrated *behavior that is followed by a positive consequence will tend to repeat itself,* we should try to discover if our nonperformance problems are occurring because nonperformance is being rewarded.

It is clearly evident that one of the reasons workers don't do what they are supposed to do is because they receive more reward for not doing it. Amazing as it may seem, frequently it is the manager who rewards the worker for not doing it the way the manager wants it done. This occurs because most managers interpret what is happening to subordinates in view of how they, the managers, view the world, not how the subordinate views the world.

For example let's take a look at a worker with an absentee problem. From the boss's point of view the worker appears to be capable of doing the job; he may even have done it well at one time. Because of the high absentee rate, however, the boss is now unable to assign important jobs to the worker. The boss spends a lot of time talking to the worker trying to get to know him better, to understand his motivation. The boss discusses loyalty, teamwork, personal growth toward building a future with the company, and has even asked the worker which jobs he would rather have. In the boss's eyes the worker is unreliable. Because of this unreliability there is certainly no future in the company for this worker. This unreliability gives the worker a low value in the manager's eyes, and if the problem is not cleared up, it will eventually lead to the worker being fired. The boss cannot understand how anybody can go through the world doing such a thing. If he were to be absent for obviously unimportant reasons he wouldn't be able to face himself in the mirror.

Now let's look at it from the worker's point of view.

1. When I take days off I get paid for not working (company sick pay policy).
2. I can sleep later on days I don't work, and do lots of other interesting things rather than work.
3. I get a lot of attention from the boss.
4. They put me on the easy jobs (which are not hampered by absenteeism.)

5. They keep talking to me, but they don't fire me (it usually takes a year around here).

You can see how the consequences visualized by the worker are personally relevant, immediate, and positive, whereas the consequences to the worker as visualized by the boss are either irrelevant, long range, or actually positive to the worker. You may feel I am pushing you back into the mind-reading business, but I am not. The problem is not difficult if you restrict your understanding of consequences to the work environment. You really know more about that than you think you do.

For example, if you have worked in business for any amount of time you must be aware of the unwritten rule, *if you have important things to do, go to the people you can count on.* This is frequently demonstrated when a boss needs something important done. The more critical the task, the more likely the boss will seek the most capable subordinate to do it. The boss is certainly being logical in using the source where services will be rendered, and avoiding the source where experience has shown that services will not be rendered. It's the essence of survival.

Unfortunately, the boss is assisting in the metamorphosis of individual workers, permitting them to do little, with the positive consequence that they will be asked to do less in the future. They are learning *the less you do the less you are asked to do.* This occurs at all levels in the organization. When it occurs at the higher levels it appears almost obscene that someone should be paid $40,000 a year to do relatively nothing.

Efforts are not being made to solve the problem; it is just being avoided. The avoidance is nonetheless resulting in positive consequences to the worker for nonperformance. In some companies the positive consequence of nonperformance is to be sent off to a seminar. I don't mean seminars designed specifically to teach a skill to correct a performance problem caused by a skill deficiency. I mean seminars that are nonskill oriented and fall under the general heading of *development*.

In discussing performance-appraisal design with the Canadian division of a worldwide company, the director of human resource development was lamenting the scarcity of transfers of high-potential managers between divisions, although these transfers meant promotions for the individuals.

He said, "Each division is willing to give us candidates to fill these promotion positions, but they do not give us their best people. When we ask for their best managers, as indicated by previous performance records, the division heads always come up with reasons why they can't let the individuals go." "As a result," he said, "I know we are not getting the best men for these promotions. We are only getting those people they feel they can spare, and in some instances people they are happy to get rid of. The real high-potential managers are being locked into their divisions and the acceleration of their personal long-range development is being slowed."

This is not an isolated incident. It happens to a greater or lesser degree in all organizations, whether it be business, governmental, or academic institutions. The individual managers making these decisions are following the logic of their survival rules. They are keeping what they believe to be the high-level talent in their own lifeboat to insure their own survival, and willingly shifting the dead wood to anyone else who will take it. These decisions are perfectly logical to the managers making them. The consequence is that nonperformance is being rewarded by promotion, and performance is being punished by no advancement.

Another example of nonperformance being rewarded occurs under the mistaken heading of something called teamwork. In one college library one of the tasks that every member of the staff had to perform was called *reading the shelves*. The library was divided into sections, and each staff member was assigned a section. *Reading the shelves* required the staff member to read the numbers on every book on the shelves in his section to insure the books were in their proper numerical sequence. It took approximately four hours to complete a section and the head librarian required it done weekly. The staff members considered it a boring, detestable job.

By noon each Friday the head librarian checked a chart on which staff members were supposed to indicate whether or not they had done their assigned shelf reading. Frequently he discovered that various staff members, with the excuse of having too much work to do, would not have completed, or even begun, their shelf reading assignment. The head librarian would respond by asking other staff members, who had completed their sections, to do the *shelf reading* for the members who didn't do theirs. There were staff members who accomplished their shelf reading every week, and there were staff members who did shelf reading only two out of every three weeks. No one was ever fired or reprimanded for failing to do his shelf reading. The consequence of not doing your assigned shelf reading was to have someone else do it for you.

In one of my seminars a manager asked, "How do you handle a secretary who complains about the work she has to do, although the work load is not heavy and she has plenty of time to do it?" He explained that, although the secretary was hired to work for two sales managers, only one was on the staff when she was hired. During the eight weeks it took to hire the second sales manager, the secretary's work load was approximately half of what you might consider to be normal. Soon after the second sales manager arrived however, she complained that the workload was unreasonable. As he described it, first she complained to either or both of the sales managers and then began to complain to the people near her work area. Now, he said the problem is worse; she spends a lot of time away from her work station complaining to other people in the office about her heavy work load. He assured me there were no conflicts in priorities, and the work she had to do was not unreasonable because they both travelled quite a bit.

When I asked him what the sales managers did when the secretary first complained he replied, "Well, the first few times they listened to her complaints and then gave her flowers. But that had no effect, the complaints were increasing rather than decreasing." I asked him to analyze this problem in view of the behavior management concept *all behavior is a function of its consequences.* He quickly recognized that the receiving of flowers by the secretary was obviously a positive consequence to her, and was reinforcing her *complaining behavior*, because it was increasing. I told him if they kept giving her flowers every time she complained they would most likely have her out on the street stopping traffic, complaining to strangers about the unreasonable work load. The managers were doing what they thought was nice, but they were actually rewarding non-performance. They should have brought her flowers on those occasions when she did not complain about the work load.

This is an amusing example of managers effectively using positive reinforcement to increase the frequency of a behavior they didn't want. The fact is that positive reinforcement increases the probability of a behavior repeating itself independently of the intent of those who dispense the reinforcement and those who receive the reinforcement. For example, have you ever had discussions with subordinates about their nonperformance in which you discussed their poor attitude and stressed the need for them to change, but they didn't change. In fact you found yourself holding more discussions about attitude. This happens when you play amateur psychologist because your attention is very likely a positive consequence to the subordinate. In effect your attention may be reinforcing *excuses and promises to change,* leaving the troublesome behavior unchanged. Your behavior may increase the likelihood that the subordinate will offer excuses and promises to change when the nonperformance again occurs.

One sales manager described a problem salesman who was invariably late with certain required periodic reports. The manager's tactic to correct this problem was to ask the problem salesman to stand up in the monthly group sales meeting and explain why his reports were late. This would usually be accompanied by joking and laughter from other salesman. The problem salesman would be on his feet five to ten minutes talking about himself, his territory, his work, and why the reports were late. The manager's logic was that embarrassing the salesman in front of the other sales people would eventually result in getting the reports in on time.

The manager did this for almost a year with no change in the lateness of the reports. He said, "It was hard to believe but the problem salesman always had some plausible sounding excuse for his late reports." Then, for some reason, the manager did not get around to using that tactic at three consecutive monthly meetings. At the end of the fourth month, all the required reports were submitted on time. The manager said he had complimented the salesman in private on one occasion about the on-time reports and never had trouble with late reports again. He couldn't understand why.

As frequently happens, managers' actions they construe as negative consequences may actually be positive consequences to subordinates. Standing up in front of a group and being the center of attention amidst friendly banter is a positive consequence to a lot of people, not a threat.

If your analysis of "What is influencing poor performance?" leads you to the conclusion that POSITIVE CONSEQUENCES ARE FOLLOWING NONPERFORMANCE, the solution is, CHANGE THE CONSEQUENCES. Remove the positive consequence for nonperformance, and arrange for positive consequences to follow performance.

COULD SUBORDINATES DO IT IF THEY WANTED TO?

Let's assume that in your analysis to determine what is influencing poor performance, you determined the following:

The subordinate knows that performance is not satisfactory.

The subordinate knows what is supposed to be done and when.

There are no obstacles beyond his or her control.

The subordinate knows how to do it.

A negative consequence does not follow performance.

A positive consequence does not follow nonperformance.

Therefore, you are at the point where you must make a judgment about the subordinate, in response to the question, "Do I believe this subordinate could do this task if he or she wanted to?" The implication of this question is that if you stuck a gun in his ear and threatened to pull the trigger if he didn't do it, would he do it? Usually, this is the first question managers ask when faced with nonperformance. They immediately answer it, "Of course the SOB could do it if he would get off his tail." The manager then proceeds with the Y, S, and T approach to get the subordinate off his tail. Unfortunately, the question, and its answer, have value to guide your management actions only if they are preceded by the analysis outlined above.

If the answer to this question is "no," the only alternative is to TRANSFER OR TERMINATE THE SUBORDINATE (unless you decide to live with the unsatisfactory performance). If your decision is to live with it, you might wonder why you bothered about it in the first place.

COACHING ANALYSIS: What is influencing unsatisfactory performance?

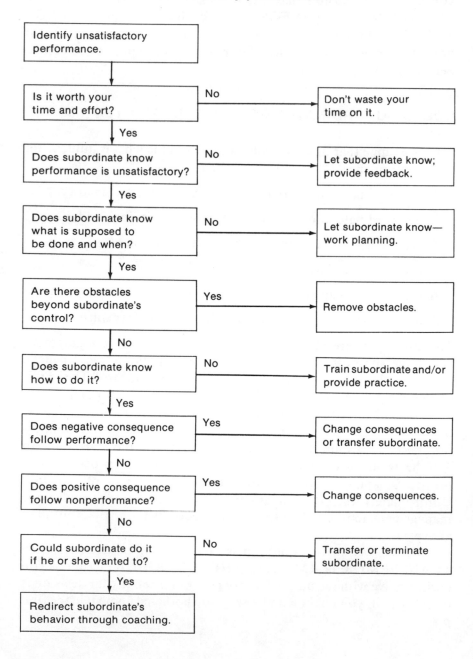

If this decision seems too final to you, all I can say is, "Learn to live with the performance problem because you can't do anything about it." It is certainly possible that you hired someone incapable of doing the job or too mentally ill for you to manage (personal limits). There may also be influential variables in their private lives that are beyond your and their control to limit or to counterbalance. If you have correctly applied the coaching analysis and arrived at the conclusion *they can't do it,* you have no other alternatives as a manager.

If the answer is *yes, they could do it if they wanted to,* the appropriate alternative for you is to REDIRECT THE SUBORDINATE'S BEHAVIOR THROUGH THE COACHING DISCUSSION, described in the next chapter.

9
Coaching: The Face-to-Face Discussion

The primary purpose of the face-to-face process, called coaching, is to redirect a subordinate's behavior to solve a performance problem: to get the subordinate to stop doing what he shouldn't be doing or to start doing what he should be doing. The assumption is that you have completed your coaching analysis, which has left you with the conclusion that the subordinate COULD DO IT IF HE OR SHE WANTED TO.

If you have not completed the coaching analysis you should not be holding a coaching discussion. The coaching discussion will not be effective if nonperformance is occurring because of the reasons given in the coaching analysis. The coaching discussion is effective in redirecting behavior only when other obstacles have been removed. For example, if someone does not know how to do something (skill deficiency), you will not be able to get him to do it (redirect his behavior) unless he learns how to do it. Sometimes during your coaching discussion you may discover something you overlooked in your coaching analysis. For example, you may learn there is an obstacle you didn't know about, which is preventing performance. Stop the coaching discussion at that point and proceed as you would in the analysis, i.e. remove the obstacle.

Preparation for the coaching meeting should be similar to preparations you have undoubtedly made in the past for appraisal discussions:

1. Hold it in some private place so the conversation cannot be overheard.

2. Do not have a third party present if at all possible.
3. Take steps ahead of time to insure there are no interruptions, phone calls, etc.
4. Do not hold it in a restaurant. No matter how good it feels, there are too many distractions to be successful. For the same reason, don't hold it in a car while one of you is driving.
5. Allow as much time as it will take so you don't have to end the discussion before you have completed it.
6. Do not start the coaching meeting until you are able to control your emotions.
7. Have a specific description of the behavior discrepancy that is going to be discussed. If you are going to talk about tardiness, you should have accurate information, such as the specific incidences of lateness and the amount of time late, as related to scheduled work days as well as to the norm or average for other workers.
8. Be prepared to substantiate logically the importance of the desirable performance, as well as the nonperformance. You are pursuing the coaching process, obviously, because you believe the nonperformance is important.
9. Determine in advance that it is the subordinate's behavior that will affect the desired change in performance. Obviously, if the subordinate's performance doesn't affect the change, why should you talk to the subordinate about that problem?
10. Decide ahead of time what minimum action you will accept as a result of this meeting; what the possible alternative solutions are; and when you expect performance to improve.

STEP 1—GETTING AGREEMENT A PROBLEM EXISTS

The first step in the coaching process is to GET AGREEMENT A PROBLEM EXISTS. This is the most critical step in the coaching process, and usually will involve half of the total time spent in a coaching discussion. This first step is where most managers fail in their efforts to eliminate performance problems. They fail here because they bypass it. It is a natural tendency for managers to assume the subordinate knows a problem exists. "After all," they explain, "it is the subordinate who is doing the thing wrong; therefore, he must know what he is doing." It sounds logical, but it doesn't work that way. As pointed out in the discussion of feedback, a common cause of nonperformance is that subordinates frequently are doing one thing but think they are doing something else. They are not aware their performance is less than expected. Even more difficult to believe, though true, is that subordinates may know they are doing something wrong, BUT THEY DON'T KNOW IT'S A PROBLEM.

Most managers believe that two people cannot collaborate in solving a business problem unless they agree a problem exists in the first place. The only reason this logical and most important first step is bypassed with subordinate problems is because managers assume the subordinate knows the problem exists.

A good example of this was described by an executive of a small chemical company who told me he was going to fire one of his staff, a Ph.D. chemist. The chemist's performance was satisfactory, except he rarely submitted weekly progress reports to the executive although the executive repeatedly requested them. According to the executive, "I have been trying to get him to submit these reports for over a year now with no success. If he can't do something as simple as that, it's not worth the aggravation to me to keep him; there are enough Ph.D. chemists on the market."

I taught him the coaching process and suggested he try that before he incurred the expense of replacing his chemist. A month later he told me he used the coaching process and was amazed to discover why the chemist was not submitting the reports.

According to the executive, during the first step of the coaching discussion, GETTING AGREEMENT THE PROBLEM EXISTS, the chemist related that because he and the executive met informally each day to discuss progress, the chemist assumed the written reports were merely a clerical detail and not necessary. The chemist said, "I thought you knew everything that was in the reports anyhow so there seemed no necessity to give you a written one." The executive informed the chemist that he did not know enough in spite of the verbal briefings. "Although the verbal reports were informative," the executive said, "I need the complete information between covers so I can study it, remember it, and refer to it as necessary."

The chemist apologized for assuming the verbal briefings were a substitute for written reports, and agreed to submit them thereafter.

The executive told me that in the three weeks following the coaching discussion, he had received three weekly reports without any further discussion. He was confident he would continue to receive them.

This is a common occurrence and a good example of the importance of the first step in the coaching process. The chemist knew he was not doing something, BUT HE DIDN'T KNOW IT WAS A PROBLEM. The important part of this first step is not telling people there is a problem or doing something called *letting them know there is a problem*, it is actually GETTING THEIR AGREEMENT A PROBLEM EXISTS. The only way to know you have achieved this is when the sounds coming out of the subordinate's mouth sound something like this, "Yes, I agree that is a problem."

You will use up approximately 50 percent of all of the coaching time in this first step. In fact, you may believe you have spent too much time on this first step, and proceed to Step 2, even though you did not get agreement. Don't do it, because you will not succeed in solving the problem if the subordinate does not agree it is a problem. If the performance discrepancy you are working on is really not important, you will not be able to get the subordinate to agree it is. This points out an additional reason for a realistic answer to that important question at the beginning of the coaching analysis, "Is it worth your time and effort?"

There are only two reasons that convince a subordinate a problem exists:

1. If the subordinate perceives the results or outcome of what he or she is doing wrong or failing to do right, or
2. If the subordinate perceives the consequences to himself if there is no change.

The results referred to in Number 1 are those things that happen in the world to the people around them because of the subordinate's nonperformance. For example, a subordinate's nonperformance might interrupt service to someone who needs it; others might not be able to do their jobs because of late prework; extra work might be required; additional costs might be incurred; damage or injury might occur; customers might complain; and your boss might yell at you.

The consequences in Number 2 refer to those things that will happen to the subordinate if the subordinate doesn't eliminate the nonperformance. For example, certain prestigious work normally assigned to the subordinate may be given to someone else; the subordinate may be transferred, fired, or demoted; he may not receive a raise; he may be denied preferable assignments; he may be removed from membership on prestigious committees; he may be denied attendance at certain enjoyable things such as conventions or remotely related business travel and nonskill seminars. Obviously these consequences will vary widely depending upon the subordinate's job.

The consequences under Number 1 clearly relate to what is happening to everybody else because of the subordinate's nonperformance, while the consequences in Number 2 are clearly what could happen to the subordinate if he or she doesn't stop it.

You may conclude that the consequences under Number 2 sound quite punitive. You are right, although punishment is not our intent. If you relate this to our earlier discussion of George Kelly's ideas, you will recall our conclusion was *people do not go through the world doing self-destructive things on purpose.* If they select what they believe to be the best alternative from those *they see* available to them at that particular time, then what they are doing must seem like a great idea to them, even though we know it is self-destructive. If you believe that people do not do self-destructive things on purpose, it is quite appropriate for you to assume if you can get people to recognize the consequences of things they are doing wrong, they will agree it is a problem.

The practical result of using this coaching process in business is that 95 percent of the nonperformers will agree there is a problem once they recognize the results of the thing they are doing wrong. Ninety-five percent of that remaining 5 percent will agree there is a problem once they recognize the consequence, or what is going to happen to them if they don't stop it. People do not do self-destructive things on purpose. If they do them they either don't know the consequences will be self-destructive to them, or they don't believe those consequences will happen to them.

You will note that the percentages above do not lead you to believe there is going to be a 100-percent success with this process. The simple fact is that you cannot control all the consequences influencing your subordinates. On occasion elements of nonperformance will be supported by positive consequences beyond your control. You will not be able to save everybody. You will fire some employees. Some subordinates will realize, because of your more specific efforts in managing their behavior, that they no longer can dazzle you with fast footwork, and they will resign.

Let's consider what these consequences might be for an employee named Herman, who is frequently late for work. You have defined *frequently late* in this instance as three late arrivals every five days, compared to an average lateness of one per month for everyone else. The results of nonperformance as they might occur under Number 1 are as follows:

A. His phone rings and is not answered, so callers are not serviced.
B. Callers who don't get an answer call someone else (possibly higher level) and complain.
C. At times other workers interrupt their work to answer Herman's unattended phone.
D. The work of others is delayed because Herman's work does not begin on time.
E. Other workers complain about alleged preferential treatment. (Why isn't everybody required to come to work on time?)
F. Your boss questions your ability to get your subordinates to come to work on time.

Depending upon Herman's specific job, your list may not include all of these, and may include some that are not listed. What is important is that the results you define are real rather than imagined.

Now let's consider consequences that might occur under reason Number 2 if there is no change. In this particular instance they might be as follows:

A. As continued lateness reflects unreliability, Herman may be barred from a promotional opportunity.
B. Herman may have to be transferred to a lower-level or less responsible job.
C. You may have to terminate Herman and replace him with someone who will come to work on time.
D. Failure to follow the rule to come to work on time may bar him from a salary increase.

You can see that some of these consequences may be beyond your control, but there are things that will happen to Herman you will initiate. You do not have a choice whether or not you permit Herman to come to work late. It is a company rule that you didn't make; you just have to administer it. Ignoring it is not an alternative. Now if you tell Herman that he must come to work on time and he refuses to come to work on time, he is restricting the alternatives available to you.

As discussed earlier, neither you or your subordinates have unlimited alternatives of behavior available on the job. Both your behaviors are restricted; each job has specific behaviors that are appropriate to that job. When a subordinate does not do what he is supposed to do, your behavior as a manager is even more restricted. It is the subordinate's behavior that dictates your behavior. For example, you may know with certainty that if Herman's lateness continued and you recommended him for a promotion or a raise, the boss would not only refuse to approve your recommendation but would question why you would do that for someone who refuses to come to work on time.

In some instances there may be only one consequence under reason Number 2, such as, "If he doesn't stop it you are going to have to replace him with somebody who will come to work on time." If you do not have a choice to permit him to continue to be late for work, your alternatives are limited.

Your objective in listing these results and consequences of the non-performance is not to dream up horror stories to scare the people who work for you. You don't want to scare them, you just want to help them. You want to help them stop their self-destructive behavior by letting them know the consequences of that behavior. Remember, we believe that people will always select what they believe to be the best alternative from those alternatives they see available to them. The reasons people do what appear to be illogical things at work, things that turn out to be self-destructive behavior is because 1) they do not truly know what the consequences are, 2) they overestimate their ability to escape the consequences, or 3) they don't know what else to do.

Let's go back to our example of Charlie stabbing his mother-in-law. If, when Charlie was about to plunge the bread knife into his mother-in-law's throat, we had grabbed his wrist and said, "Charlie, do you realize you could end up in jail for the rest of your life if you do this?"

Charlie: But she's driving me crazy and I have to shut her up.

> We: Is there any other way you can shut her up besides stabbing her?
>
> Charlie: She would probably shut up if I punched her in the mouth.
>
> We: Would you go to jail for life if you did that?
>
> Charlie: No, they would probably just get me on assault and battery, and I might get thirty days.
>
> We: Which sounds like the better alternative?

Charlie's most likely response is that he will drop the knife and punch his mother-in-law in the mouth.

In our lateness example, the fact is that Herman is involved in self-destructive behavior. It is destructive both to the organization and to Herman. Because you are trying to eliminate self-destructive behavior, you must identify the consequences of this destructive behavior and the consequences if it doesn't change. You must know what they are before you begin your coaching discussion.

Whatever the consequences may be, it is not enough that they exist, it is necessary they be perceived by the subordinate as the result of inappropriate behavior. The quickest and most effective method to get the subordinate to perceive these consequences, and for you to know this perception has occurred, is for the subordinate to *tell you* what these consequences are. You accomplish this through thought transmission using the questioning techniques to make sounds come out of his mouth.

Let's deal with your subordinate, Herman, whose *coming-to-work-late behavior* you have identified as inappropriate. Let's also assume you have gone through the steps of the coaching analysis. You let him know what was expected as *on time* reporting to work and what might be considered as allowable tardiness. You gave him feedback about his tardiness. You determined there were no obstacles beyond his control; there are no negative consequences of getting to work on time; and no positive consequences, within your control, following tardiness. You know Herman possesses the skill to be able to come to work on time, so in your judgment *he could do it if he wanted to.*

Therefore, you decided to use the coaching discussion to redirect his behavior. All of your efforts in the coaching discussion will be based on a few important assumptions, like these:

I don't believe Herman realizes how his lateness affects the rest of the organization. Secondly, I don't believe Herman realizes what the consequences are if he doesn't stop coming to work late. As soon as he realizes this, I am sure he will do what is necessary to get to work on time. If he doesn't know what to do I will do everything possible to increase his alternatives.

Your conversation should proceed something like this.

> You: Do you know why I've called you in?
>
> Herman: No.
>
> You: I've called you in because we have a problem.
>
> Herman: What problem?
>
> You: It's about your performance.
>
> Herman: What about my performance? I thought I was going pretty good. After all you gave me a raise six months ago. Besides I think I turn out a lot more work than anybody else in the department.
>
> You: It has to do with your not coming to work on time.
>
> Herman: Oh, that. Yeah, I know I have been late a few times. I was wondering when you would get around to it. I'm sorry about that. I'll clean it up.
>
> You: Do you know how many times you have been late in the last six months? (You can use whatever period you are concerned about.)
>
> Herman: Probably more than I should, but like I said I'll take care of that.
>
> You: I'm glad you are willing to take care of that, but do you know how many times you have been late in that period? (Note the positive response as positive reinforcement to his desirable reaction "Going to take care of this.")
>
> Herman: I have no idea.
>
> You: Guess.
>
> Herman: Probably once or twice a week every few weeks.
>
> You: Based on the number of work days during the period, which is ...., you were on time only 40 percent of the time. This averages out to three days late per week.
>
> Herman: I didn't realize it was that many days.

NOTE: If he had not responded after one or two minutes, you could have asked, "What do you think about that?"

> You: Do you agree that it is a problem? (You are trying to get his agreement that a problem exists.)
>
> Herman: I agree it's a lot of days, but after all I work harder than anybody else so it all evens out.

NOTE: He obviously doesn't agree it's a problem. Because he has not agreed it is a problem it is necessary for you to do what it takes to get him to perceive the results of his unsatisfactory behavior.

> You: When you are late for work do you know how late you usually are?
>
> Herman: I have no idea.
>
> You: Guess.
>
> Herman: Five to ten minutes.
>
> You: Would you like to know how much it really is?
>
> Herman: Yes, *or* You mean it's worse than that?
>
> You: It varies from . . . to . . . with an average of . . . . (Keep silent and wait for his response. Look at him with expectation).
>
> Herman: I had no idea it was that bad, *or* As I said already, I am going to clear it up.
>
> You: It is helpful that you are willing to clear this up (positive reinforcement); does that mean you agree it is a problem?
>
> Herman: I am willing to clear it up, but, as I said before, I don't think it is a problem when you consider the amount of work I do compared to everybody else.
>
> You: Do you know what happens when you don't come to work on time?
>
> Herman: Well, I guess you get mad at me.
>
> You: Not mad, just disappointed. Do you know what else happens when you don't come to work on time?
>
> Herman: Well, I heard some grumbling that some of the other people out there don't like answering my phone when I am late for work.
>
> You: You're exactly right. What else happens?
>
> Herman: Well, I have had some calls from our customers who seemed a little teed off that they couldn't get me first thing in the morning.
>
> You: You're right. What else happens?
>
> Herman: I can't think of anything else.
>
> You: There's no rush. I'll wait while you think about it.

Herman: (Probably after several minutes of silence.) I guess data processing gets delayed in some of their work when I hand in my previous day's reports thirty minutes late in the morning.

You: That's right. What else happens?

Herman: (Perhaps after several minutes of silence.) I really can't think of anything else.

You: If people who call you early in the morning get no answer what do you think they do?

Herman: They call back later.

You: What else might they do?

Herman: They call someone else.

You: Right. What do you think they might say to someone else because they couldn't get you?

Herman: I guess they would complain.

You: You're exactly right. I have received several phone calls and people have complained.

Herman: I didn't know that.

You: Do you think there might be a reaction from other employees who usually come to work on time?

Herman: I guess they could interpret it as unfair treatment that I don't come to work on time.

You: You are right. Several employees have expressed concern about what they feel to be partial treatment for you.

Herman: I didn't know that.

You: Do you know what happens to me frequently when you are late for work?

Herman: No.

You: Did you know that my boss knows when you are late?

Herman: I guess he does since he walks through here every morning.

You: You are right. Do you know what he does when you are not at work when he walks by?

Herman: No.

You: Guess.

Herman: He chews you out.

You: You are exactly right. He wants to know why I can't manage my people to get them to work on time.

Herman: That figures, *or* That's logical, *or* I am sorry about that.

NOTE: You have just used up reason Number 1 as to why the subordinate should agree that a problem exists, so ask the big question.

> You: Now don't you agree that it's a problem?
> Herman: Well, I guess when you put that all together I suppose it is a problem.

NOTE: Hooray! You just got through Step Number 1, GETTING AGREEMENT THAT A PROBLEM EXISTS. Now you are ready for Step Number 2, which is *mutually discussing alternative solutions.* But what if Herman hadn't agreed it was a problem and had responded as follows:

> Herman: Well, I understand all those things happening but I still don't think it's a problem because I do more work in a day than they do anyhow. You told me at review time six months ago that I hardly ever make any errors and that my productivity was the highest in the department. If I get my work done, why are you hassling me just because I don't get to work on time?

NOTE: OOPS! Reason Number 1 didn't do it. If what he says to you sounds like a good argument, it would be logical to let him off the hook. But I might ask why you didn't decide that before you got started, before you wasted your time and Herman's time. Now you look like a fool. Stop the discussion and don't get involved in the future unless IT REALLY IS WORTH YOUR TIME.

If you must decrease the lateness, however, proceed with reason Number 2, *Consequences if he does not stop it.*

> You: Let me ask you a question. What do you think will happen if you continue to come to work late?
> Herman: Well, I guess you'll get more complaints from people who call early.
> You: You're right. What else?
> Herman: The boss will get on your back.
> You: You're right. He'll convince me that I'm in trouble as a manager. What else?
> Herman: I guess the people around me will still complain.
> You: You're right. They'll probably complain more and ask for

somebody to do something about it. Some of them may
even come in late. What else?

Herman: You could fire me.

You: You're right; I need somebody in that job who will do
what has to be done and I wish it were you. Now don't
you agree that this is a problem?

NOTE: Everytime the consequence of firing comes up always repeat
the statement "I need someone in that job who will do what has to be
done and I wish it were you."

By now you might have concluded that this conversation is threatening to Herman. Well, you are right. Nevertheless, there is a clear difference between your actually threatening to take his job away from him,
and his recognizing the consequences of *his own behavior.* Threats per
se usually do not work. Sometimes the threatened worker responds
with a resignation on the spot. If termination of employment is a realistic consequence of the subordinate's unsatisfactory behavior (self-
destructive behavior), then it is important (and only fair) that he or she
be made aware of that consequence. People are free to act as they
choose as long as they are aware of the consequences of that action. It
is only reasonable that your workers accept responsibility for their
own behavior. Their behavior limits alternative behavior available
to you.

The likely response after these consequences have been verbalized is
that the subordinate will agree a problem exists.

Herman: Yes, I agree that it's a problem.

You: I'm glad you recognize the problem. How can we solve it?

NOTE: Hooray! You have just finished Step 1 and begun Step 2,
which is MUTUALLY DISCUSS THE ALTERNATIVE SOLU-
TIONS. But what if Herman's response was this:

Herman: I don't think it's fair that you are going to fire me just
because I am late for work; after all I produce a lot more
for you.

You: Let me ask you a question. Do you think I can decide to
let you come to work late?

Herman: Yes, you could if you want to, *or* I think you do, *or* I don't
know.

You: I can't; I have no choice. We are talking about a company rule that is beyond my control. Not only that, but the element of fairness requires that all of the employees follow certain rules. Now let me ask you another question. If I tell you that you must come to work on time and you don't do it, what alternative decisions do you think are available to me?

Herman: You can do anything you want; you are the boss.

You: No, I can't. Your behavior restricts my behavior.

Herman: Well, you could fire me.

You: That's right. I need somebody in that job who will do what has to be done, and I wish it were you. What else?

Herman: You could demote me.

You: Yes, that's right. What else?

Herman: I don't know anything else.

You: Now if all these things could happen to you because you are not coming to work on time, don't you agree that it's a problem?

Herman: I guess you are right. If I am really going to lose my job because I come to work late, then it is a problem.

You: I'm glad you agree it's a problem. Now how are we going to solve it?

NOTE: Hooray! You have just finished Step Number 1 and now are proceeding to Step Number 2: MUTUALLY DISCUSS THE ALTERNATIVE SOLUTIONS. But let's not make this too easy; suppose he still will not agree it's a problem, and this is what he says:

Herman: I don't think it's a problem; you are making a mountain out of a mole hill.

You: I am puzzled. (Follow this with silence, but look at him with the expectation that he is going to respond.)

Herman: Puzzled over what?

You: Well, I just told you I don't have a choice to permit you to come to work late, and you just told me that if you continue to come to work late that you could be demoted or lose your job, yet you still don't agree that it's a problem. That's what puzzles me. (Followed by silence.)

Herman: Well, I just don't think it's fair blowing my lateness all out of proportion.

You: I can recognize that you think it's unfair, but don't you agree that it's a problem if all those things will happen to you because of it?

Herman: Yes, it's a problem, but it's not fair.

You: Well, I'm glad you recognize it's a problem, now how are we going to solve it?

NOTE: Hooray! You just finished Step Number 1 and are now into Step Number 2.

An interesting point you might raise here is why we pursued this so far, when, in the beginning of this discussion, the subordinate indicated his willingness to correct it. I can explain by asking you: "If someone is doing something inappropriate now, and he does not think it is a problem or important, what makes you think he will begin to do it appropriately?

A common complaint of managers is that subordinates frequently promise to eliminate a nonperformance problem, but they don't. The only short cut to Step Number 1 is if you called somebody in and the discussion went something like this.

You: Do you know why I called you in here?

Subordinate: Yes, I believe you called me in because I have been late for work quite a bit lately. I know it creates a problem to the people around me, as well as the people I service. I am going to correct it.

You: Do you agree that it's a problem?

Subordinate: Yes, I agree that it's a problem, and I am going to do everything to correct it.

NOTE: Hooray! You just finished Step 1, GETTING AGREEMENT THAT A PROBLEM EXISTS, and you are ready for Step 2.

One good question that may occur to you is: "What do you do if you can't get a subordinate to agree that a problem exists?" This will rarely occur if you have done your homework before beginning the coaching discussion. If it does occur, however, it is likely that it will have happened for these reasons:

1) You are not dealing with a behavior.

2) What you are dealing with isn't really important.
3) It is important, but you have not identified all of the consequences under Reasons 1 and 2.
4) You are trying to get the subordinate to recognize unrealistic consequences or hypothetical consequences, which are not likely to occur.
5) You are not using thought transmission; instead of the consequences being verbalized by the subordinate you are verbalizing them, and the subordinate is nodding his or her head or merely saying *yes* or *no*.
6) Your past relationships with your subordinates have proven to them that you threaten a lot but never do anything about it.
7) There is a positive consequence for the subordinate if he or she is fired.
8) The subordinate is too mentally ill to be managed.

STEP 2—MUTUALLY DISCUSS ALTERNATIVE SOLUTIONS

The next step in the coaching discussion is to mutually discuss alternative solutions. In this step you and the subordinate together will identify as many alternative solutions as may be necessary to solve the problem. Because experience is merely increasing the number of alternatives an individual has to select from when faced with a requirement to act, this step actually compresses experience for the subordinate; it increases his or her alternatives quickly. Because you are dealing with behavior, it is necessary to specify those changes in behavior that are needed to influence the outcome or result. The subordinate may not know what to do to solve the performance problem.

For example, if the nonperformance problem you are working on is *increased typing errors*, you will get nowhere if the solution is to *decrease typing errors*. Effective alternative solutions might be:

1) type slower,
2) don't leave typing for the last thing to be done each day,
3) stop typing if people stop by to gossip,
4) wear your glasses in the office,
5) proofread each page before handing it in, rather than proofreading as you type it,

6) proofread it by asking somebody else to read it while you check for errors, or
7) identify the errors you make most often and slow down when you get near one.

I don't propose all of these alternatives are necessary to decrease somebody's typing errors, but one or more might be. For example, possible alternative solutions to Herman's lateness problem might be as follows:

1) set the alarm clock early enough,
2) buy an alarm clock that works,
3) get an alarm clock with a louder alarm,
4) put the alarm clock far enough away from the bed so Herman must get out of bed to shut it off,
5) catch an earlier bus or train,
6) drop out of the car pool that usually arrives late,
7) get to bed earlier during the work week,
8) change babysitters to one who shows up on time, or
9) get the car fixed so it will start in the morning.

Again all of these solutions will rarely be needed to solve a late arrival problem, but I hope you are surprised there can be that many possible alternatives. It is important to recognize that whatever the subordinate is *doing now* results in his late arrival at work. What he is doing is not working. Therefore, the purpose of the second step is to identify WHAT THE SUBORDINATE COULD DO DIFFERENTLY SO THAT HE WILL ARRIVE AT WORK ON TIME.

Many discussions about performance problems end when the subordinate says, "Okay, boss, I'll try harder." And the boss responds with something like, "I am glad to hear that." The boss believes the problem is solved. It is certainly nice that the subordinate will try harder, but the question is: WHAT WILL HE DO DIFFERENTLY SO THAT WHEN WE SEE IT WE WILL KNOW HE IS TRYING HARDER?

Unfortunately, we have many workers who try harder, but are still doing the wrong thing. That is, they are doing *more of* something, but what they are doing will not result in solving the problem. Unless you specify what *trying harder* is, the only result you may achieve is people walking around with clenched fists, tight buttocks, and grinding teeth. It will certainly give them a feeling of trying harder, but they will not be doing anything to change the outcome.

It is important to recognize that Step 2 is not a *selection of alternatives*, but just the listing of what the possible alternatives might be. The selection of specific alternatives from those available will be accomplished in Step 3. In Step 2 you may list nine possible alternatives to solving the problem, but in Step 3 you may select only two of them.

The *mutual* aspect of this step relates to the expectation that both of you will contribute to the solutions. You should assume that the subordinate will be able to come up with some solutions to solve the problem. But if he or she is unable to, it is up to you to furnish the necessary solutions. You can best accomplish this step using thought transmission, making the sounds come out of his or her mouth.

You can not begin Step 2 until Step 1 has been completed. You will know that Step 1 has been completed when the subordinate says something like, "Yes, I agree that's the problem." You then begin Step 2 as follows:

You: I am glad you agree; now how are we going to solve it? (This is a good time to smile and recognize progress.)

Herman: Well, I'll come to work on time.

You: That's good, but what will you do differently?

Herman: Like I said, I'll get to work on time.

You: If what you are doing now is getting you to work late what will you have to do different so you will arrive at work on time?

Herman: I don't know.

You: Well, what do you do now that results in getting you to work late?

Herman: Well, I turn my alarm clock off in the morning and go back to sleep.

You: That's a good clue. What will you do differently?

Herman: Well, I'd stop it if I knew I was doing it, but I don't realize I'm doing it when I do it.

You: What do you mean?

Herman: Well, when the alarm goes off, I reach out and shut it off while I'm half asleep, and then I roll over and go back to sleep.

NOTE: The solution you have in your head is that he should place the alarm clock far enough away from the bed so he has to get out of bed to shut it off. But you want to use thought transmission to communicate this, so you say:

> You: What would happen if you couldn't reach the alarm clock?
> Herman: But I can reach it.
> You: I know that, but what would happen if you couldn't reach it?
> Herman: You mean if it were someplace across the room?
> You: Yes, that's right.
> Herman: Well, I guess I would have to get up and turn it off.
> You: What would happen if you had to get out of bed to turn it off?
> Herman: Well, I would have to be awake to be able to do that, and I guess if I did that I wouldn't go back to sleep without knowing it.
> You: That sounds like a great idea. What else could you do to get to work on time?
> Herman: I can't think of anything.
> You: Well, what else do you do now that results in your getting to work late?
> Herman: Well, the car doesn't start some mornings and I have to get somebody to give me a push.
> You: Why is that?
> Herman: In the cold weather the battery doesn't work too well.
> You: Why is that?
> Herman: Well, I guess it's an old battery.
> You: What's the solution to that?
> Herman: I guess I should get a new battery.
> You: That's a great idea. What else can you do to get to work on time?
> Herman: I can't think of anything else. Those are the only problems I have.

NOTE: If in your judgment you have mutually discussed sufficient alternative solutions to solve the problem, you have completed Step 2. You are ready to go on to Step 3.

STEP 3—MUTUALLY AGREE ON ACTION TO BE TAKEN TO SOLVE THE PROBLEM

The next step in the coaching discussion is to gain mutual agreement on which alternatives previously discussed will be acted upon to solve the problem. As mentioned earlier, the mutual discussion of possible alternatives is entirely separate from the selection of alternatives that will be acted upon.

A common practice managers follow in their problem-solving efforts is to combine the selection of alternatives with the listing or discovery of alternatives. Unfortunately, these are two clearly separate functions; combining them inhibits the optimum achievement of either. If you argue the merits of ideas as they are given, you are wasting *idea-giving time.* If you reject ideas as they are given you could be punishing *idea-giving behavior*, thereby decreasing idea-giving. Of course, you could reinforce idea-giving by recognizing good ideas when they come up, but the common trap is to stop searching for ideas when a good idea comes up, and before all the ideas come out. The process of generating ideas depends on the interaction of ideas. The best ideas are rebounds from bad or trivial ones. Finally, when you select ideas as they are given, you inhibit idea-giving because a worker may not want to act on certain ideas. So he rejects the idea, not because it is a bad idea, but because he doesn't want to do it. When this occurs it would be appropriate for you to state that your intent at this point (Step 2) is not to state actions that will be taken later, but only to list possible alternatives.

In Step 3 you will not only mutually agree on which alternatives will be acted upon, but will also specify when the action will take place. You want to identify *what* will be done and *when.* Again the best technique for accomplishing Step 3 is thought transmission.

When you complete Step 2 (in your judgment all solutions necessary have been discussed), you begin Step 3 as follows:

> You: What are you going to do to solve the problem? (Followed by silence.)
> Herman: What we said.
> You: What's that?
> Herman: I'll move my alarm clock away from the bed so I can't

reach it, so I have to get out of bed in the morning to turn it off.

You: That's great. Do you have an idea where you will put it?

Herman: Yes, I'll put it on my dresser.

You: How far away is that?

Herman: Oh, that's about eight feet away.

You: That sounds like a great idea. You certainly are going to have to be awake to walk eight feet to turn it off.

Herman: That's what I thought.

You: What else will you do?

Herman: That's all for now.

You: But didn't you tell me that one of the reasons you are late is because you can't get your car started on cold mornings?

Herman: Yes.

You: What are you going to do about that?

Herman: (Silence.)

You: (After a minimum of one minute's silence.) What was the possible solution you mentioned a minute ago?

Herman: I said a new battery would solve the problem.

You: That's right; so what are you going to do?

Herman: I guess I am going to have to buy a new battery.

You: That's great. That will solve that problem. When are you going to do it?

Herman: First chance I get.

You: That's great. When is that?

Herman: I haven't thought about it.

You: Take a minute to think about it. (Followed by silence.)

Herman: I don't have the money to buy it.

You: When will you have enough money?

Herman: If I save $2 a week I will have enough money in about fifteen weeks.

You: That's not an alternative; we can't wait that long to solve this problem. What else could you do?

Herman: But I don't have the money.

You: When do you think this tardiness problem has to be solved?

Herman: Right away.

> You: That's right. But what do you mean by right away, today,
> tomorrow, or the end of the week?
> Herman: I guess if I solved it by the end of the week it would be okay.
> You: That's right, so when do you need a new battery?
> Herman: By the end of the week.
> You: That makes a lot of sense. So what will you do?
> Herman: I guess I can buy a cheaper battery on pay day.
> You: That sounds like a great idea.

NOTE: You just got commitment as to *what* will be done and *when* as solutions to solve the problem. An appropriate closing response would be to thank the subordinate for agreeing to solve the problem, and to specify a time when you will meet again:

> You: I am glad you have agreed to solve this problem. Thank
> you for your efforts. I'll see you tomorrow morning at . . .
> (whatever the starting time is).

STEP 4—FOLLOW UP TO INSURE THAT AGREED UPON ACTION HAS BEEN TAKEN

The second most common reason for manager failure in all functions at all levels is lack of follow-up. It is also one of the most common reasons managers fail in their efforts to correct subordinates' unsatisfactory performance. It never ceases to amaze me that managers will take the time to chew on subordinates about a problem, but will not take the time to insure the agreed upon action has been taken. What usually happens is that the manager is overwhelmed by the subordinate's *promises to change*. The subordinate has confessed his error, has expressed the right amount of humility and thoughtful concern, and has reaffirmed his loyalty to the crown; therefore, the manager assumes the change will take place.

This sounds reasonable because we are not dealing with children; we have two mature (sometimes educated) and experienced people dealing on a face-to-face basis. We have to assume there is still some honor and integrity left in the world, so we take the subordinate at face value and assume that what is expected to happen (or promised) will occur. Too often we discover, three months later, things are just as bad as they were in spite of the subordinate's promises. It really does happen that, although subordinates promise to make changes, they really don't change, and it takes the boss three months to find out.

But what happens sometimes is the subordinate *does* change initially and, because the boss does not follow up, there is no recognition of this change and, therefore, no reinforcement to support the change. So the subordinate returns to the inappropriate behavior. The manager taking a look at the scene three months later just assumes no change has ever ocurred. Logic would have to tell you what the subordinate is doing unsatisfactorily must feel good to the subordinate. If he changes and does it the way you want it done, you have to be there to make it feel good or he will go back to the old way.

There are also occasions when the manager will adroitly follow up immediately following the subordinate's promise to change, but will not follow up thereafter. Following up only once is better than nothing, but it will usually have the same result as no follow-up: a return to the unsatisfactory performance.

There are those managers who do not believe that follow-up is a part of the management process for a myriad of reasons. There are also many managers who tried to follow up at one time, but stopped doing it because they could not defend what they were doing to their subordinates. When initial efforts to follow up with subordinates result in a confrontation, the manager usually decides to avoid it in the future. Some typical responses from subordinates when a manager follows up are:

"What's the matter, don't you trust me?"

"Look, if you think I'm not able to do this job, why don't you take it away from me; otherwise just let me do it."

"Look, if you don't have confidence that I can do this job, why did you give it to me in the first place?"

"If you don't like it when it's finished, tell me then, but let me work on it in peace."

"I wish you would treat me like the professional I am, rather than checking up on me all the time."

Managers do not know how to respond to these comments. Although most management-training programs tell managers *they must follow up*, the subject is never covered in sufficient detail to explain the *why* and the *how*, or even *what it is*. So let's see if we can clear up some of the confusion here.

The first important point is to know what follow-up is. FOLLOW-UP IS THE PROCESS OF FINDING OUT WHETHER THE SUBORDINATE IS DOING WHAT HE IS SUPPOSED TO DO. The important prerequisite is that you and he both know what it is that is supposed to be done, which includes how much of it will be done when, and what it is supposed to look like if the right amount is done at the right time. To convince you this is not double talk, let's relate it to a performance problem. For example, let's assume the performance discrepancy you are trying to solve with coaching is an excessive absence from the work station, and you have gotten the subordinate to agree that he will decrease his absence from the work station. The next step, of course, is for you to follow up tomorrow to find out whether he has done that. Obviously, you will observe him several times tomorrow to determine whether or not he is at his work station. But supposing I ask you:

Me: How will you know if the problem is corrected?

You: He will not be absent from his work station.

Me: You mean he will never be absent from his work station?

You: Well, he has to be absent sometimes to take a coffee break or go to the restroom. After all, there are times when it's okay to be absent from his work station.

Me: That makes sense. Well, how many times is it permissible for him to be away from his work station before you will say the problem is improved?

You: I haven't thought of a specific number, but just so it's better than what it was.

Me: That sounds logical. What was the average number of times he was away from his work station each day?

You: Well, I don't have an exact number, but it would be more than anyone else.

Me: Well, how many times is normal for everybody else?

You: I think about three or four times each day.

Me: Is that an exact number based on your observations, or is that what you think it ought to be?

You: Well, I can't stand around and observe people all day long. I just think that's probably what it ought to be, with a coffee break in the morning and a coffee break in the afternoon and maybe one or two unscheduled visits to the restroom.

Me: Okay, how many more times a day than three or four was the problem subordinate away from his work station?

You: I don't know exactly, but it seemed like he was gone everytime I passed his work station.

Me: Do you have a record of how many times you passed his work station and how many of those times he was not there?

You: Of course not. I have more important things to do than sit around keeping records on that sort of thing.

Me: But if you don't know how often he was away from his work station, how will you know if it gets better?

You: Well, he will just be there whenever I pass his work station.

Me: But you just said that under normal conditions he could be away from his work station three or four times a day.

You: Well, I mean if he's away from his work station other than those three or four normal times.

Me: That sounds reasonable. Does the subordinate know how many times it is okay to be away from his work station?

You: Well, we didn't talk about that specifically.

Me: That brings us back to the basic question. If neither you nor the subordinate knows specifically what is the allowable number of times and when it is allowable to be absent from the work station, how will either of you know when the subordinate is doing what is expected?

You: You mean I have to be *that* specific?

Me: No, you just have to be specific. If you don't know the appropriate numbers of absences or the appropriate times when allowable absences from the work station could occur, how will you be able to determine whether or not the subordinate is doing what is supposed to be done?

You: You mean I should specify that allowable absences from the work station are no more than two times in the morning and two times in the afternoon, and two of those times may be coffee breaks not to exceed fifteen minutes and two of those times can be unscheduled breaks not to exceed ten minutes?

Me: That sounds great. Now both you and the subordinate know what acceptable performance will look like when you see it.

As strange as this conversation may seem to you, it occurs numerous times when I discuss performance problems with managers. It is easy for managers to tell subordinates to *shape up, get with it,* or *start earning your pay*, but without defining specifically what it is supposed to look like, neither the manager nor the subordinate will be able to recognize improved performance when it occurs.

If you had really progressed to Step 4 in the coaching process, you would have had more facts than you appeared to have in the conversation above. For example, in order to identify the performance discrepancy of excessive absence from the work station you would have had to take a little work sampling. You would have had to pass by his work station at fixed intervals each day and then record the number of times you had observed that subordinate away from his work station, compared to the other subordinates. After several day's observations you would have known that the other workers averaged three to four absences per day, while the problem subordinate averaged six to eight absences. Without that information you couldn't have gotten the subordinate to agree there was a problem.

Many managers who know what follow-up is, don't know the reasons for it. In other words, they confuse the reason for follow-up as being synonymous with the definition of follow-up, i.e., the reason I want to know whether people are doing what they are supposed to do is because I want to know whether people are doing what they are supposed to do. That is good stuff to know only if you do something about it. The two reasons for follow-up are:

1) If people are doing what they are supposed to, the manager must *recognize* those achievements.
2) If people are not doing what they are supposed to do, the manager does one of the most important reasons for being on the payroll and that is to ask, "How can I help?"

In coaching when you follow up and observe that a problem worker has improved, you must recognize that improvement by saying something like, "I see you have corrected that problem. I really appreciate your efforts on that. If you keep that up, pretty soon it will go away all together. Thank you very much." The sounds coming out of your mouth recognizing his achievement reinforce the increase in that specific activity. This is quite different from saying to yourself, "Well, I see the SOB did it right at least once."

The second reason for follow-up invariably escapes most managers. If they meet with a subordinate to engineer corrective action, and their follow-up reveals nonperformance, their typical reaction is, "That SOB is still screwing up."

Remember the earlier, obvious conclusion we drew was: THE ONLY REASON YOU ARE THERE AS A MANAGER IS TO DO EVERYTHING WITHIN YOUR POWER TO HELP YOUR SUBORDINATES BE AS SUCCESSFUL AS POSSIBLE. Therefore, if your subordinate is continuing to fail, your additional help is needed. That help may be in the form of providing additional alternatives because the ones selected didn't work, or it may be using your organizational influence to clear away obstacles, or it may be merely to clarify further *what is expected to be done when, and how it will be recognized.*

Therefore, when subordinates accuse you of treating them like children because you follow up, just explain to them what follow-up is, and tell them you have no choice. If you didn't follow up, you would be involved in self-destructive behavior as a manager.

One critical aspect of the follow-up process is timeliness. If you are playing amateur psychologist and dealing with changes in attitude, it is necessary to observe many behaviors over a long period of time to establish a basis for your guesses about the attitude. Likewise, if you are dealing with sales results and cost figures, you will most likely be unable to follow up until the appropriate computer run comes out at the end of the month or quarter. Both of these lead to ineffective follow-up because they are not soon enough.

Because the coaching process directs your corrective efforts to specific behavior, you don't have to wait too long for the opportunity to observe that behavior in the normal work environment. For example, in our problem with Herman, if "*on time arrival*" for work is the promised behavior change, the next work day is the first time you would expect to observe that behavior. The more specifically you define the behavior that must change, the easier it is for you to determine whether or not the change has taken place. If he does arrive on time it is important for you to be there. The conversation might go something like this:

> You: Herman, I see you came to work on time today. Thank you. Tell me, did you move your alarm clock last night?
>
> Herman: Yes, I put it over on the dresser.

You: That's where you said you were going to put it. How did it work this morning?

Herman: Well, I got out of bed to shut it off and I felt like jumping back in bed again, but I said to myself, "Well, I'm up now I might as well stay up."

You: That's great, Herman. I see you are really making an effort to solve this problem.

NOTE: Let's suppose it's now the day after pay day and he was supposed to buy the battery for his car. The appropriate time for you to follow up with him would be the first work day after pay day. That conversation might go something like this.

You: Good morning, Herman; I see you came to work on time again. Tell me did you buy that battery over the weekend?

Herman: Yes, I did. I got one on sale and it didn't cost me as much as I thought it would, and I installed it over the weekend.

You: How did it work this morning?

Herman: It wasn't too cold, but the car really kicks over now.

You: That's great, Herman. I am really glad to hear your car is running better, and I want to thank you for the efforts you are making to clear up this tardiness problem. Keep this up and your record will be back to normal.

NOTE: This is not the end of it; your follow-up must be scheduled to examine on time behavior weekly or monthly until you conclude that this behavior is a part of Herman's customary behavior.

STEP 5—RECOGNIZE ANY ACHIEVEMENT

The last step in the coaching process has the greatest potential to sustain improvements in performance; that step is RECOGNIZE ANY ACHIEVEMENT when it occurs. The complimentary sounds that come out of your mouth concerning his behavior are a recognition of his achievement, which is a vital part of your efforts to correct nonperformance problems. The influence of your recognition of achievement is of such major importance in the coaching process it is treated as a separate step.

The timeliness of your recognition is of critical importance to its influence on sustaining improvement. The sooner recognition (reinforcement) occurs after the actual performance achievement, the greater is its influence. The longer the period of time between the actual performance and the occurrence of the reinforcement, the less influence it has. For example, if your intended follow-up was to check Herman's time card daily, but not to recognize any improvements verbally unless he had perfect attendance at the end of the month, it is not likely you will get 100 percent punctual behavior for the month. You will not be doing anything to reinforce daily improvement.

If someone corrects something today, it is better to thank him face-to-face today than to send him a memo a week from now expressing your appreciation. If someone working for you at another location corrects performance by sending in his report on time, it would be more effective to call him when you receive the report than to thank him the next time you meet him, weeks later. If someone corrects a performance problem today it is more effective for you to tell him about it this week, than to give him a raise eight months from now and tell him at that time how much you appreciated it. If someone must improve his performance today, which will result in a change on the computer print out next month, it is more effective to call him today to find out whether he did it or not, and if he did it, to recognize his achievement during that phone call. If someone is supposed to behave differently at 10 o'clock today, and he does it, it is more effective if you recognize that change at 10:15 rather than at 5:00 tonight or tomorrow. The guide you should follow in recognizing any achievement is: WHEN IN DOUBT DO IT NOW.

Unfortunately most managers working to correct performance usually expect it to go from failure to perfection in one jump. A subordinate failing by 15 percent who shows only a 5 percent improvement is still considered by the manager to be failing by 10 percent. Obviously there is nothing to recognize because failure is still occurring. But you will recall, from our discussions of Herzberg's theory, that individuals are not motivated by failure, they are motivated by achievement. Individuals experiencing little bits of achievements are motivated to try more bits of achievements. What this means to us in business is that if someone failing by 15 percent manages to improve his performance by 5 percent, and you recognize that 5 percent improvement, you have a greater chance of getting the other 10 percent improvement. If this is so, why would any manager choose to ignore the 5 percent improvement? That would be self-destructive behavior.

In the example with Herman, you will recall that late arrival occurred three out of five days per week. Therefore, if after your coaching discussion Herman was late only one day per week, that would be an improvement. It does not mean the entire problem is solved, but it does mean you should recognize the level of improvement that has taken place. By doing so you are using the most appropriate means of achieving total improvement.

An appropriate statement you could make at the end of the week where only one lateness had occurred (rather than three) might be as follows: "Herman, you have improved your performance. You came to work on time almost every day this week, four out of the five days. If you keep this up pretty soon you will be coming to work on time every day, as we planned. Thank you." Your complimentary remarks will function as a positive reinforcement to increase the frequency of *on time behavior.*

Behavior management research has demonstrated that positive reinforcement is more effective if it is not continuous; that is, if it does not occur each time performance occurs. As a matter of fact, studies have shown that when reinforcement is continuous the behavior being reinforced will cease to occur once the reinforcement is removed. Once somebody has changed his *late arrival* behavior to *on time arrival,* your recognition would cease to have the effect of reinforcement. If you frequently thank someone who normally comes to work on time for coming to work on time, his likely response would be, "Why are you doing that? I come to work on time all the time." When the desired behavior change becomes a part of the individual's repertoire, and occurs with normally expected frequency, your reinforcement should decrease.

The most effective schedule of reinforcement would be intermittent scheduling. For example, you may be observing punctual behavior daily, but you should reinforce it only the first two days, then twice each week for three weeks, then once each week for four weeks, and then, perhaps, once each month for several months.

CONTINGENCY RECOGNITION

Another form of recognition is a positive consequence within your sphere of influence you prearrange to happen to the subordinate when the behavior improvement occurs. For example, in Step 3 of the coaching discussion, when you are getting agreement on what actions will take place to solve the problem, you may tell Herman if he can arrive on time for the next sixty days, you will assign him certain important and desirable projects. This would establish a contingency relationship between a specific reinforcement that Herman will receive and his behavior, when it changes appropriately. It is important this positive consequence you promise actually is a positive consequence to Herman. What you construe to be important work may be just *more work* to Herman. Secondly, if a contingency is promised you had better deliver when the time comes.

Contingency recognition is not a new concept to managers. Unfortunately, they use it as a con job. For example, managers hand out sticky jobs to subordinates and mention should the subordinate do this sticky job well, the boss will remember the subordinate come raise time twelve months from now. There is nothing wrong with that until two months later when the boss hands out another sticky job to the same subordinate and again promises if it is done well the reward will come at raise time. Is the boss increasing the anticipated raise increment each time he hands out a sticky project, or is he really promising the same raise several times?

Managers would be a lot more successful if they recognized they are insulting the intelligence of their subordinates by promising the same reward for several jobs. Even more important, there are other things in a manager's sphere of influence that have nothing to do with spending money, but are more effective as reinforcers because they can be administered immediately. Here are some contingency recognitions of achievement that cost a lot less than a salary increase.

"If you complete this report on time, I will give you the next easy job that comes into the department."

"On any day you produce zero errors, you can go home a half hour early."

"If you can keep your cost within budget for six months, I will take you to the convention."

"If you meet all your schedules, I will give you the next new executive chair we receive."

"If you will stop arguing with that department, I will move your desk closer to the window."

These are just some examples to trigger your thinking. If you tried you could very quickly make up a list twice as long.

If you know that a consequence within your sphere of influence is a positive consequence to your subordinates, consider it in Step 3 as a possible recognition to the subordinate, contingent upon his changing his behavior. But make certain you and the subordinate agree on how and when performance improvement will be recognized. Otherwise, your contingency agreement will lead to arguments and conflict rather than a reinforcement of a desired behavior.

Although recognition of achievement is part of the follow-up process it has been treated as a separate step in the coaching process because of its vital importance. If you do not recognize a subordinate's change from unsatisfactory to satisfactory performance, you will not sustain the change; you will have wasted your time. Only when you have achieved a sustained change, have you completed the coaching process.

STEPS OF COACHING TECHNIQUE

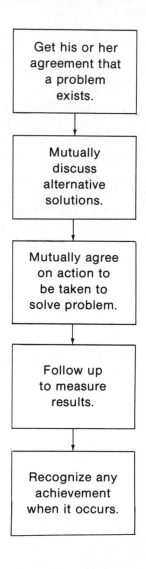

10
But What If
It Doesn't Work

One logical question you might ask at this point is: But what if he is late to work the very next day, then what do I do?"

You should undertake a new coaching discussion, except the problem this time is not *coming to work late*, it is *not doing what he said he was going to do*. The conversation may go something like this.

You: Do you know why I called you in?

Herman: Yeah, I know I was late to work, and I'm sorry. I'm not going to do it again.

You: That's not why I called you in.

Herman: Then why did you call me in?

You: We have a problem.

Herman: What's the problem?

You: Let me ask you a question. Did we have a meeting last night?

Herman: Yes.

You: What was it about?

Herman: About my coming to work late.

You: Did you agree that it was a problem?

Herman: Yes, and I said I was going to change it.

You: What did you say you were going to do?

Herman: I said I was going to come to work on time this morning.

You: Did you?

Herman: No.

You: That's the problem. You didn't do what you said you were going to do.

167

Herman: I know. I'm going to come to work on time tomorrow.

You: Let me ask you a question. If you don't do what you say you are going to do, what basis do we have for an employment relationship?

Herman: I know I promised, but something came up and I'm going to come to work on time tomorrow.

You: Please answer the question. If you don't do what you say you are going to do, what basis do we have for an employment relationship?

Herman: You mean if I don't tell you the truth how can we work together?

You: That's right.

Herman: Well, I guess there is no basis for the relationship.

You: You are exactly right. If there is no basis for a relationship, what happens to you?

Herman: Well, I guess I get fired.

You: That's right! That certainly could happen. Now don't you agree that's a problem?

Herman: Yes, I agree that's a problem, and I told you I am going to come to work on time.

You: Well, I'm glad you agree it's a problem. How are we going to solve it?

Herman: I am going to do what I said I was going to do.

You: What's that?

Herman: I'm going to come to work on time.

You: When?

Herman: Tomorrow.

You: I'm glad you have agreed to solve this problem. I'll see you tomorrow. Thank you very much. (End of conversation.)

Now you ask: "But what if he doesn't come to work on time tomorrow?" You should conduct the same coaching discussion again, but when the subordinate promises he will come to work on time the following day, you ask one additional question, as follows:

You: Let me ask you a question. What will happen if you don't come to work on time tomorrow?

Herman: Then I guess you and I will be talking again.

You: No, we won't. What else could happen?

Herman: I don't know.

　You: Guess.

Herman: Do you mean I'll get fired?

　You: You have agreed that if you don't do what you say you are going to do we have no basis for a work relationship. So if tomorrow, for the third time, you don't do what you said you were going to do, how can that relationship continue?

Herman: You mean if I don't come to work on time tomorrow I am fired?

　You: That's right.

Herman: You mean I am going to lose my job in spite of what I do for you only because I come to work late three days in a row?

　You: No, it's only because for three times in a row you said you were going to solve a problem and three times in a row you did not do what you said you were going to do. There are not many alternatives available to me if the people who work for me don't do what they say they are going to do. I don't have a choice.

Herman: Well, I guess you are right. You don't have anything else you can do.

　You: You are exactly right. Your behavior controls my behavior. Now what are you going to do about it

Herman: Well, I'm going to come to work on time.

　You: I'm glad you agree to solve the problem. Do you know what's going to happen tomorrow if you don't come to work on time?

Herman: Yes, I am going to get fired.

　You: Yes, if you don't come to work on time tomorrow that means you are not doing what you said you were going to do and I will assume that since you know there is no basis for our relationship, that it doesn't matter to you if the relationship is terminated.

If in actual practice someone promised three times he would behave in a certain way and three times in a row he did not, it would be my guess that on the fourth try he will also not do it. Therefore, you will be terminating that subordinate's employment with the company. You may conclude that since the purpose of the coaching process is to improve unsatisfactory performance rather than fire employees, the coaching process has failed. I would certainly agree with you on that. You should not assume that if you use coaching you will never have to fire anyone. But you could assume that with the proper use of the coaching technique you will be firing fewer people, not because you will learn to live with nonperformance but because you will correct nonperformance problems quickly.

In the above situation, an employee may be fired after four daily efforts to correct performance. This is in contrast to what I currently see happening in business, where the same employee might fail for eight months and then be fired. The time would be longer, but there would be a lot less functional effort to solve the problem than has occurred in the four days of coaching. In both instances, the employee was fired, but in one instance it took eight months to discover the situation was not correctable. As mentioned earlier in the book, when you hire someone you do not buy his body or his mind, you only rent his behavior.

When someone whose behavior you are renting chooses not to deliver what you have rented, there is no basis for a work relationship. Because you are dealing with behavior rather than internalized attitudes and motives, neither you nor the subordinate can evade your corrective efforts. Because you are dealing with behavior, it is most likely that behavior must occur in the next work day. If it does not occur it is clear the subordinate did not do what he said he would do. If your union contract precludes terminating employment without written warnings, you would have given three warnings in three days.

One sales manager, relating his first experience in coaching a salesman, said it resulted in the salesman's resignation. In the middle of the coaching discussion, the salesman interrupted the discussion by saying to the manager, "I guess I don't really want to work as hard as I have to work in your company to fill this job. So I might as well resign." I asked the manager whether this was a good or bad result from coaching. His response was, "It was good and bad. It was bad because it gave me an open territory and I lost a salesman, but it was good because it eliminated that salesman then. Under normal conditions without the coaching process, I would have agonized over his performance problem for another six months before he either resigned or I fired him."

You will end up firing some subordinates and some of them will quit, but you will have a lot more confidence you did everything possible to correct the problem. There will be times when you will not get a change in behavior because *you failed* in the coaching process. Let's suppose Herman promised to come to work on time the following day; you were there to greet him (follow-up), but he was late for work again. When he finally arrived he said, "Gee, boss, I wanted to be on time, but my alarm clock didn't work."

Surprise! The reason you didn't get improvement is because in Step 2 of the coaching process you didn't actually identify what the subordinate HAD TO DO DIFFERENT to arrive at work on time. You didn't discover the other influences preventing punctuality, the malfunctioning clock. For example, at the end of Step 1, when he agreed there was a problem, the discussion should have been like this.

> You: I am glad you agree that a problem exists. But what are we going to do about it? (Step 2 beginning.)
>
> Herman: Well, I'll just try harder to come to work.
>
> You: That's great that you are going to try harder, but tell me what are you going to do differently.
>
> Herman: Well, gee, I do everything I possibly can now.
>
> You: Why are you late for work?
>
> Herman: Well, sometimes my alarm clock doesn't go off.
>
> You: I see. How could we solve that? (Of course you know how but you have to make the sounds come out of his mouth.)
>
> Herman: Well, I guess I could buy a new alarm clock.
>
> You: That's a good idea. What else goes wrong?
>
> Herman: Well, lots of times the person I ride with doesn't show up.
>
> You: What could you do about that?
>
> Herman: Well, I guess I could find somebody else to ride with.
>
> You: That's a good idea. Is there any other reason you don't come to work on time?
>
> Herman: Well, I guess a lot of times I go to parties during the week and stay out too late because I am having such a good time. Then I hate to get out of bed in the morning.

You: What can you do about that?

Herman: Well, I guess I could go to fewer parties or come home a little earlier during the week.

You: That's a good idea. Is there anything else you can think of?

Herman: I can't think of anything else.

NOTE: If you can't think of any other alternative solutions you have just finished Step 2, and you should begin Step 3.

You: They sound like good solutions. Now which of those are you going to do?

Herman: Well, I am going to buy a new alarm clock.

You: Good idea. When?

Herman: Right away.

You: When is that?

Herman: On my lunch hour.

You: That's a good idea. What else are you going to do?

Herman: Well, like I said, I'm not going to go to as many parties and I'm going to get home earlier.

You: How much earlier do you think you need to get home.

Herman: Well, I haven't thought about it.

You: Okay, I'll wait while you think.

Herman: Well, I guess I ought to be home before 1 A.M. If I get home any later than that, I usually don't want to get up in the morning.

You: Getting home by 1 A.M. sounds like a good idea. What else are you going to do?

Herman: Well, I'm going to change the person I ride with.

You: When will you do that?

Herman: Well, that may take me a little time. I will have to ask around, and I don't know exactly how to go about it.

You: Do you think the personnel department might know who lives in your area?

Herman: Yes, it might be a good idea to call them.

You: Yes, I think that will work. Do people looking for rides sometimes advertise?

Herman: Yes, they put a little blip in the company newsletter. I could probably do that.

    You: That sounds like a good idea. Is there anything else you
         could do?
Herman: Well, I see notices on the bulletin board sometimes with
         people asking for rides. I guess I could do that.
    You: That's a good idea.

NOTE: Your alternative solutions should counteract the reasons for
nonperformance if possible.

When your initial follow-up reveals a cause for nonperformance
that could be counteracted by an alternative solution, resume your
coaching discussion at Step 2. But during that same coaching process
you should also try to uncover any further influences preventing
punctual behavior. You should discover then, and not two days later,
that additional reasons for occasional late arrival may be the car pool
or partying.

When you have identified *who* was going to do *what, when*, to solve
this problem, you are ready to go on to Step 4, which is FOLLOW-UP.
If the subordinate said he was going to buy a new alarm clock at lunch
time, your follow-up step should be to see him after lunch to find out
whether he did in fact buy a clock. If he did, you can recognize his
action. You should follow-up similarly on his actions to call the personnel department; to place an ad in the newsletter; and to put a notice
on the bulletin board. The remainder of your follow-up efforts relate
to his arrival for work.

We could go on and play the game *but what if* forever and still not
cover all the possibilities you might be faced with. The important point
is that this methodology permits you to adapt your approach to the
specifics of each situation. It is not necessary for you to solve every
influential nuance in an individual's life to achieve a simple behavior
change such as arriving at work on time. If you use the coaching process to get Herman to agree that a problem exists and you reinforce
any punctual arrival for work, the result very likely will be that he will
buy the clock, eliminate the car pool problem, and come home from
parties earlier without you discussing it. The only reason we went into
that much detail is to provide you with some alternatives to the *but
what if* problems.

Tardiness was chosen as the first example because it appears to be
one of the most frequent problems managers have difficulty solving.

Excessive absenteeism is also a common problem. If you substitute the absence problem for the tardiness problem with Herman, the approach would be quite similar, although there are other influences that may interfere. For example, one company has a policy of providing workers with twelve paid sick days per year. Their policy does not permit workers to accumulate sick days. If the twelve days are not used by the end of the year, the worker loses them. If you analyzed this problem with coaching analysis it would be clearly evident that one of the positive consequences of being absent one day per month is to have a day off and be paid for it. (Nonperformance is rewarding.) Also, the negative consequence of coming to work every day is to lose twelve day's pay that you are entitled to. (Performance is punishing.) The result is that the majority of the employees in this company are absent from work ten to twelve days per year. It is common knowledge that people use the sick days to do many things besides being sick. In some departments it is common for people to call in and say, "I am taking one of my sick days."

The managers try to keep absenteeism below twelve days per year, but when they pressure employees who have missed seven or eight days before the end of the year, the employees claim the managers are in conflict with company policy and have no right to set up a different policy in each department. The managers tell me their hands are tied. The employees are only taking advantage of a company policy; it would be highly ridiculous for them not to.

Certainly you could undertake the coaching process to get agreement that a problem exists, but you do not have the alternative of the ultimate consequence of termination until the employee exceeds the twelve sick days that are allowed.

One manager in that company asked me what was the most serious consequence he could use in his coaching discussion with someone who was missing nine or ten days a year. The manager wanted to correct the problem because she thought the subordinate would be in line for promotion sometime in the future. I asked her what the average absenteeism was for the supervisors and managers in her organization. Her reply was three to five days per year. My suggestion was that her discussion of the consequences with that subordinate go something like this:

She: Do you know what the average absenteeism is for the workers?

Sub.: Probably twelve days a year.

She: You are right. Do you know what the average absenteeism is for supervisors and managers?

Sub.: I don't know.

She: What would you guess?

Sub.: A lot less?

She: You are right. It's no more than five days per year. Now are you interested in being a candidate for future promotion?

Sub.: Of course.

She: What do you think are some of the things management looks at when deciding to promote someone?

Sub.: Work performance.

She: Yes, what else?

Sub.: Reliability.

She: You are right. Do you know how we measure reliability?

Sub.: No, but because you brought it up, I guess absenteeism has something to do with that.

She: You are right. It has a lot to do with it. Let me ask you a question. Suppose I have one promotional position available and I am reviewing two subordinates for that promotion. With all else being equal, one of them has an absenteeism of twelve days per year, and the other has an absenteeism of let's say, five days per year. Which one do you think I'll choose?

Sub.: You would probably choose the one with five days per year.

She: You are exactly right. Now don't you agree nine to ten days absence is a problem?

Sub.: Yes.

The most practical way to solve this company's absentee problem would be to change the consequences, by changing the policy. For example, if the policy were changed to permit people to accumulate sick days forever, rather than to lose them each year, the consequences to the individual worker would change. The consequence of coming to work every day would be a positive consequence of adding to the individual's bank account of sick days that would be available in the future should a major illness occur. The consequence of taking twelve sick days a year when you really didn't need them would be a negative consequence of wasting paid days for sick days that were not needed. If the policy were changed, frequent periodic reports should be given to each worker showing their current accumulated bank account of sick days. This problem points out the importance of the coaching analysis to identify important influences that support nonperformance.

11
Coaching Cases

Let's run through another coaching discussion, this time without all the interruptions. In this case, which happens to be a real one, you are a sales manager. Your company has recently introduced a new product that is a substitute for a former product. Although the new product is available for sale you still have considerable inventory of the former product. About a month ago, you called all your salesmen together and asked them to help clean out the inventory of the old product by selling it before they sold the new product. At your request, they all agreed to sell a specific amount within the next ninety days. Thirty days later, the sales figures showed that everybody was selling the older product except Jack, your star salesman. He had high sales for the month, but all his sales were the new product.

At that time you called him in, told him you noticed that he had not been selling the old product, and asked him why. Jack told you he owed it to his customers not to sell them a product that was going to be immediately replaced by a new one. It was up to him to maintain integrity in his relationship with his customers. Since his customers bought a lot of product from him, he thought it would hurt his sales in the long run if he pushed the old product on them and then in sixty or ninety days announced the new product's availability. He said the company ought to bite the bullet and junk all that old product.

You told him that it was company policy to move the old product first and it was his responsibility to move his share of the older product before selling the new product. He left the meeting saying "I will try to move it if I can, but I just don't want to screw up my customers by selling that older product the company should dump anyhow."

It is now thirty days later, and the sales figures reveal that Jack is still not selling the old product. You have just finished reading this book and you want to use the coaching process to solve your problem. The symptom of the problem is that the older product is not being sold in Jack's territory. This is occurring because Jack is not presenting this product on his sales calls.

NOTE: Let's first go through the coaching analysis of this performance discrepancy to determine what is influencing unsatisfactory performance.

Question: What is the unsatisfactory performance?
  Answer: Jack is not selling the old product. He's not selling the old product because he is not presenting it to the customers when he makes customer calls.
Question: Is it worth your time and effort?
  Answer: Yes.
Question: Does Jack know his performance is unsatisfactory?
  Answer: Yes, I told him thirty days ago.
Question: Does Jack know what is supposed to be done and when?
  Answer: Yes, I told him sixty days ago in a meeting with all the salesmen and thirty days ago when I talked with him about this problem.
Question: Are there obstacles beyond Jack's control?
  Answer: No.
Question: Does Jack know how to do it?
  Answer: Yes, he outsold everybody else in that product until the new product came out.
Question: Are there negative consequences following performance?
  Answer: Although Jack says there are, there really aren't.
Question: Does positive consequence follow nonperformance?
  Answer: Yes, it is easier for him to sell the new product.
Question: Could Jack do it if he wanted to?
  Answer: Yes.

It appears that you should redirect Jack's behavior through the coaching discussion. Before you begin the coaching discussion, you must identify the results of what Jack is doing wrong and the consequences if he doesn't stop it, as follows:

What are the results of Jack not selling the old product?

a) The old product inventory is moving slowly, and the region will not meet the deadline for cleaning out the old product.
b) The other salesmen are complaining because they are selling the old product and Jack is not. They would rather sell the new product, too.
c) Your boss is complaining to you because you are not moving the old product fast enough.
d) If you don't get the old product out within the ninety days it is going to be almost impossible to sell it because of the national advertising campaign for the new product.

What are the consequences to Jack if he doesn't start selling the old product?

a) Would you fire him?
   Answer: No.
b) Would you demote him?
   Answer: No.
c) Can you transfer him into a less desirable territory?
   Answer: No.
d) Can you give him a lower raise?
   Answer: No, his high sales dictate his raise.
e) Is he interested in future promotion?
   Answer: Yes, very much so. He wants to be a national sales manager someday.

   That's great. One of the consequences of his not selling the product he is supposed to sell is that he is displaying unreliability. Part of a manager's job is doing what has to be done whether he likes it or not.

Now we are ready to begin our coaching discussion with Jack. So you set up an appointment to coach Jack and Jack has just arrived.
Step 1—GETTING AGREEMENT A PROBLEM EXISTS:

You: Do you know why I called you in?
Jack: No.
You: We have a problem.
Jack: What's the problem?

You: It has to do with your work performance.

Jack: What's the matter with my work performance? I've been carrying the highest sales dollars in the region, and I'm number three in the country.

You: The problem is you are not doing what you are supposed to do.

Jack: I guess you are talking about selling that old product.

You: Right. That's the problem. (Followed by silence.)

Jack: Yeah, I know you talked to me about that before and I was going to move it, but after all I just can't see my way clear to push that old product on customers when we have that new product out there and it's so great. It just isn't fair for the company to make us do this to our customers. We are the ones on the firing line trying to make sales happen, and the company just doesn't give a damn. Let those other guys move the old product. I'm concentrating on moving the new product, so the company can move ahead. You certainly can't complain about my sales, can you?

You: Do you know what happens when you don't sell the old product? (Notice you didn't get sidetracked.)

Jack: Yeah, I sell the new product and make just as much money for the company.

You: What else happens when you don't sell the old product?

Jack: Well I guess you get a little bent out of shape.

You: I mean what happens in the company when you don't sell that old product.

Jack: The other guys sell it.

You: That's right. The other salesmen are selling their share of the old product. Do you think they know that you're not selling it?

Jack: Well I guess they do. The sales information floats around the branch. Everybody knows what everybody else is doing.

You: You are right. They know that you aren't selling that product. Do you know what they do when you don't sell that product?

Jack: I told you they sell the product.

You: Yes, they sell it, but what else do they do when they sell it and know that you don't sell it?

Jack: I don't know.

You: What do people do when they have to do something and they see someone else who should, but is not doing it?

Jack: I guess they complain.

You: You are exactly right. They do complain. What do you think they complain about?

Jack: Well I guess they don't think it's fair.

You: You are exactly right. They don't think it's fair that they have to sell the product and you are not selling it. What else happens when you don't sell the old product?

Jack: I don't know.

You: Well, do we have a date by which the inventory of the old product should be cleaned out?

Jack: Yes.

You: If you don't sell your share, what's going to happen regarding the inventory and that date?

Jack: I guess we are just not going to have the inventory cleaned out by that date.

You: You are exactly right. We are not going to meet our regional objective for cleaning out that inventory. What else happens because of that?

Jack: I don't know.

You: Where do you think that deadline came from?

Jack: The regional manager.

You: Right. What do you think he has to say when we don't meet our deadlines?

Jack: Well, I guess he chews you out a little bit.

You: You are exactly right. He wants to know why I can't meet the company objective. Now what else do you think will happen if we don't clean that inventory out within the alloted period?

Jack: I don't know.

You: Well, if the company releases a heavy advertising program on the new product and the customers are getting smarter everyday about the new product, what will happen, let's day four months from now, when we try to sell the old product?

Jack: We won't have a chance in hell of moving the old product because the customers just won't settle for anything less than the new product.

You: You are exactly right. We will be stuck with inventory we can't move. Now don't you agree that's a problem?

Jack: Listen, I agree all those things can be a pain, but after all the objective here is to make sales happen, and I know my customers and I know my territory, and I just don't think it's right that I should destroy our relationship by pushing all that old product on them when I know I've got this great new product that will help them out.

You: (He didn't agree because of reason Number 1; now you have to go to Number 2.) Jack, did I tell you how much of the old product you had to move?

Jack: Yes.

You: Do you think I have a choice to permit you to choose to sell that product or not?

Jack: Sure you do. I'm the best salesman you have; let those other guys move the old product. Let me make bucks for the company selling the new product.

You: Would you like to know the real answer?

Jack: I suppose you are going to tell me you don't have a choice.

You: You are exactly right. I don't have a choice. I work for the company just as you do, and I take orders from the company just as you are supposed to. Now if I tell you that you have to move that old product and you don't do it, what alternatives are left open to me?

Jack: Don't tell me you are going to fire me over something that small. I'm bringing in more sales than any two other sales reps. You really need me around here.

You: That's right, Jack. I wouldn't fire you, but what other alternatives do I have?

Jack: Well, you can do anything you want. After all you are the boss.

You: No, as a matter of fact I can't do anything I want. Your behavior restricts my behavior. Let me ask you a question. We had a long conversation at the end of last year about your interest in moving up in the organization as a manager; is that still your interest?

Jack: Of course. I want to get to be national sales manager for this company. That's why I work so hard at selling.

You: Well, let me ask you another question. What are the kinds of things upper management looks at when they are trying to decide who should get promoted as a manager?

Jack: Well, I guess they look at someone who can produce, someone who can bring in the sales, someone who is intelligent and aggressive and has those kinds of qualities needed to be a manager.

You: Jack, you are exactly right. Where do you think they get that input?

Jack: Well, I guess they get it from you, from those evaluations you make and any recommendations you make about my promotions.

You: You are exactly right. What are some of the other things you think they consider when making a promotional decision?

Jack: Well, I guess they look at things like dependability, reliability, emotional maturity, and things like that.

You: You are exactly right. They do look at something called reliability and dependability. Now if I'm the one who makes comments and recommendations about your promotion, what are the kinds of things I look at as a basis for making judgments about your reliability and dependability?

Jack: Well, I guess it's whether I do the things I am supposed to do and so on.

You: You are exactly right, whether you do the things you are supposed to do. Now, if you know that you are supposed to be moving that old product and you refuse to do it, what comments do you think I must make in your folder about your reliability and dependability as it concerns promotability?

Jack: You mean you would louse up my future just because I won't move that old product?

You: Jack, you leave me no choice. Your self-destructive behavior limits my choice of behavior. If you don't do what you are supposed to do, the facts are that you are not dependable and reliable.

Jack: Boy, this is getting to be some kind of chicken outfit when a guy brings in a lot of sales and you give him a hard time just because he isn't selling some product that the company has obsoleted anyhow.

You: Jack, it's not the product we are talking about, it's your refusal to do what you are supposed to do. If you refuse to do what you are supposed to do, I don't know what else to call it except refusing to do what you are supposed to do. Now, if that's going to affect your future promotion, don't you agree that's a problem?

Jack: I think you are being unfair about this, but you are certainly right that it's going to be a problem if that's what you are going to do to me.

You: I'm glad you agree that it's a problem. How are we going to solve it? (You just finished Step 1 and began Step 2.)

Jack: Well, I guess I'm going to go out there and sell that product.

You: That's great. What specifically are you going to do?

Jack: Well, I'm going to start presenting that product to the customers instead of the new product.

You: What was our agreement at our meeting two months ago when we decided to push the old product?

Jack: We said we would sell only the old product until we ran out of it.

You: That's right. How will that influence you now?

Jack: Well, I guess I'm going to present only the old product until we run out of it.

You: That's great. But if you have sold some new product in your territory, how are you going to get over that obstacle?

Jack: That's no problem. I've got a lot of customers that I haven't sold any new product to yet, and I will just go in there and load them up with the old product.

You: Well, I am glad to see you have so much confidence in being able to move the product.

Jack: Why shouldn't I have confidence? I'm your number one salesman.

You: You are certainly right about that, Jack. (You have just finished Step 2 and are starting Step 3, which is to mutually agree on action to be taken.) Jack, what kind of a time framework do you have now that you are going to be selling that product?

Jack: Well, things look a little tight. Everybody else has been selling that product for sixty days now and we only have thirty days to go before the regional deadline for moving that product.

You: That's right. What are you going to do about that?

Jack: Well, according to my current rate of selling I ought to be able to move all of my inventory thirty days after the deadline.

You: Jack, that's not an alternative. What can you do so we can meet our deadline?

Jack: You mean you expect me to move all that product in thirty days that the other guys have been moving for sixty days?

You: Jack, the regional manager didn't give me a deadline different for you than for anybody else. They didn't tell me to treat Jack different from the rest of my people. Not only that, a minute ago you told me you are a better salesman than them, so moving that product ought to be a lot easier for you. What specifically are you going to do?

Jack: Well, if you are telling me I have no choice, I guess I have to move all of that product in the next thirty days.

You: That certainly is a positive approach. How are you going to do it?

Jack: Well, I guess I'll just temporarily delay all other sales efforts and put all my emphasis on moving that old product. I will increase my number of sales calls per day, as well as make some deals with some of my biggest customers.

You: That sounds great. How many dollars worth of sales orders will you have to write each day?

Jack: About $5,000 a day.

You: When are you going to start?

Jack: Right away.

You: When is that?

Jack: Tomorrow.

You: You mean by tomorrow night you will have brought in a minimum of $5,000 sales, and each work day hereafter you will bring in a minimum of $5,000 in sales?

Jack: Do I have any choice?

You: Is that what you are going to do?

Jack: Yes, that's what I am going to do.

You: That's great. I believe you are capable of doing that. I am pleased that you have decided to do what must be done. It looks like you are demonstrating that you have those additional qualities necessary to be a successful manager. Tomorrow night after you come back to the office, bring in your sales orders so we can discuss your production. Thank you for your time and help in working out a solution to this problem.

(You just finished Step 3. All you have to do now is Step 4, which is follow-up, and Step 5, which is recognizing achievement.)

What you just read was almost a verbatim record of a real coaching effort to solve a real problem. Jack did move all of the old product in slightly less than the thirty days left.

I hope you noted in the above dialog that the manager did not react to those salesman's comments that might be considered disrespectful, smart alecky, or as having hidden meanings. Any effort you devote to these unimportant aspects of the discussion detracts from the main objective of coaching. The purpose of the discussion is not to reaffirm Jack's allegiance to the king, but to change Jack's behavior, to get him to stop his own self-destructive behavior. In your coaching discussion, don't respond to emotional comments. Deal with the words people say, not their intent. (You can't read minds).

Let's take a look at another performance problem occurring primarily because of personal problems. You are an administrative manager, and one of your subordinates, Pete, a long-term employee has been stretching his lunch hour to two and a half hours, and appears to be drinking during it. When he comes back from lunch he smells like a brewery, and sometimes slurs his words.

When it happened the first time you didn't say anything to Pete because you felt it might be an isolated incident. If it happened only once it wouldn't be worth your time and effort. By the end of the week, however, you realized Pete did it four out of the five days. So, your first step was to have a feedback discussion with Pete to let him know his performance was unsatisfactory. You called him in Friday afternoon and told him you noticed he had been taking two and a half hours for lunch and apparently had been drinking on his lunch hour; you explain this was unsatisfactory, and you asked him to please discontinue it.

Pete's response was to tell you he had a lot of things on his mind. He related he was in the process of getting a divorce because he found his wife playing around; his daughter was coming home from college because she was pregnant; his son had just been arrested for selling pot in school; his bookie was after him because he was behind in his gambling payments; and his car needed a new transmission. Your five-minute feedback discussion turned into an hour-and-a-half crying session. You were overwhelmed by his personal problems, but you asked him to please stop taking long lunch hours and to stop drinking on his lunch hour. He said he would try, but he had a lot on his mind.

At the end of the following week you didn't talk to Pete, but you noticed he had again taken two and a half hours for lunch and had returned intoxicated four out of the five days. You decided to use the coaching process to try to solve this problem. You started with the coaching analysis.

Question: What is the unsatisfactory performance?
  Answer: Taking two and a half hours for lunch, rather than an hour, and smelling of alcohol and slurring his words when he returns to work.
Question: Is it worth your time and effort?
  Answer: Yes, if I thought this would last only two weeks I would forget about it.
Question: Does subordinate know performance is unsatisfactory?
  Answer: Yes, I told him last week.
Question: Does subordinate know what is supposed to be done, and when?
  Answer: Yes. He has been doing it for years, and I told him again last week.
Question: Are there obstacles beyond the subordinate's control?
  Answer: He has a lot of personal problems, but there is no obstacle preventing him from taking one hour for lunch and drinking less.
Question: Does subordinate know how to do it?
  Answer: Yes, he has always taken an hour for lunch in the past and rarely has more than one drink on his lunch hour.
Question: Does a negative consequence follow performance?
  Answer: No.
Question: Does a positive consequence follow nonperformance?
  Answer: Yes, he works less, and the bartender where he eats lunch listens to his troubles, but I can't change those consequences.
Question: Could he take an hour for lunch and have no more than one drink if he wanted to?
  Answer: Yes.

The logical alternative at this point would be for you to direct the subordinate's behavior through the coaching discussion. But before starting the coaching discussion, you must list the results of what he is doing wrong and the consequences if he doesn't stop it.

What are the results of Pete's long, drinking lunches?

1) His phone is not answered when he's not there.
2) Other workers answer his phone and grumble about it.
3) Other workers know what Pete is doing and are complaining about unfair treatment.
4) Because he slurs in his conversations, the people he deals with know that he drank too much.
5) Your boss told you there have been comments from executives in other divisions hinting that he is running a country club in permitting subordinates to be drunk on the job. He has told you to correct the problem or get rid of Pete.

What are the consequences to Pete if he doesn't stop?

1) You will be forced to fire him. Whatever his problems are, they are most likely going to be worse if he doesn't have a job.
2) Pete is also a special member of a management committee. If he doesn't stop, he could be removed from membership on that committee.
3) He will be prevented from attending the monthly professional meetings around the country.

Now you are ready to begin your discussion with Pete. You start with Step 1, *getting agreement a problem exists.*

You: Hello, Pete. Have a seat.
Pete: Hi.
You: Do you know why I called you in?
Pete: No, but I can make a pretty good guess.
You: What do you think it is?
Pete: Well, I guess it's about my lunch hours.
You: You are exactly right.
Pete: Well, I know I shouldn't be doing that, but as I told you, I have a lot of things on my mind lately. I have been trying not to do it, but things just get the better of me.

You: Do you know what happens when you take two and a half hours for lunch, and you act as though you had too much to drink when you return? (You can't say he was drinking too much because you weren't there to observe how much he was drinking. You were only able to observe his behavior afterwards.)

Pete: Nothing. I do my job.

You: What do you think happens when normal lunch hour is over and you are not here to answer your phone, or to see the people who come to do business with you?

Pete: Well, I guess the phone doesn't get answered, and the people have to come back some other time.

You: You are exactly right. The people who come to be serviced by you are not serviced. What else do you think happens?

Pete: Well, I don't know.

You: What do you think your fellow workers do when your phone is ringing and you are not there to anwer it?

Pete: Well, I guess they answer it sometimes.

You: You are exactly right. They interrupt their work to do your work for you. Do you think that bothers them?

Pete: Well, I don't know. I suppose it might.

You: That's right. It does bother them. What do you think they do about it?

Pete: I don't know.

You: Guess.

Pete: Well, I guess they might complain to you about it.

You: Yes, you are right. They do complain to me about it. They want to know why they have only an hour for lunch and you are able to take two and a half hours. What else happens?

Pete: Well, the heck with them. If they had as many problems as I do, they would have a lot more to worry about.

You: What else happens?

Pete: I don't know.

You: Did you know that you slur your words and appear to be intoxicated when you return from lunch?

Pete: I do not. I can hold my liquor. Besides I don't drink that much.

You: Do you know that people who have spoken to you on the

phone have complained that you sound as though you have
had too much to drink?

Pete: Well, they are full of bologna.

You: If people speak to you on the phone after lunch and you sound
to them as though you had too much to drink, what do you
think they do?

Pete: They can go stuff a chicken.

You: Do you think they might complain?

Pete: They might.

You: Who do you think they would complain to?

Pete: Probably to you.

You: Yes, you are right. Who else might they complain to?

Pete: I don't know.

You: Do you think they might complain to their boss and my boss?

Pete: Well, I guess they might do that.

You: You are exactly right. Some of them have complained to my
boss directly, and some of them have complained to their boss
directly. What do you think my boss does when that happens?

Pete: Well, I guess he gets on your back.

You: You are exactly right. He wants to know if I am running a
country club down here. Now don't you agree that's a
problem?

Pete: I just never thought the time would come when I would realize
that, in spite of the years I put into this company, it doesn't
really make a damn bit of difference. I worked my tail off and,
now when I have a few personal problems, there is just no
sympathy. All that management talk about loyalty and security isn't worth a damn when it comes down to an individual
with problems.

You: Don't you agree it's a problem?

Pete: Yeah, I agree it's a problem that the company can't meet me
halfway with my problems.

NOTE: You didn't get agreement with basis Number 1, you now have
to go to Number 2.

You: Pete, do you think I have a choice to let you take two and a
half hours for lunch, instead of one hour like everybody else?

Pete: Well, you could if you wanted to, if you had a little heart.

You: I don't have a choice. I work for the company just as you do, and I have to follow the rules, and make sure everybody follows the rules just as you do. Now let me ask you another question. If I tell you not to take two and a half hours for lunch and not to come back from lunch smelling of alcohol and slurring your words, but you continue to do so, what alternatives are available to me?

Pete: How come you are hassling me? Is it because I am old, and you want to get rid of me? I'm a good worker. I've given this company good productivity over the years, and now, when I have some personal problems, you young people just don't help me, you hassle me.

You: I am trying to get you to stop your self-destructive behavior. Because if you don't stop it, you leave me very few choices. Now what alternatives are available to me if you don't do what you are supposed to do?

Pete: You can do any damn thing you please.

You: No I can't. Your behavior limits my behavior. Now if you don't stop it, what is going to happen to you?

Pete: Well, I guess you could fire me.

You: You are right. I need somebody in that job who will do what has to be done, and I wish it were you. What else could happen?

Pete: I can't think of anything worse than that.

You: But if I didn't fire you what else could happen?

Pete: I don't know.

You: Well, you are our representative to the management committee. If you don't do what you are supposed to do, what alternatives are available to me regarding your membership on that committee?

Pete: You mean to say if I keep doing this, you are going to remove me from that management committee?

You: You are exactly right. You leave me no choice. What else could happen?

Pete: I don't know.

You: Well, you are also our representative at the monthly professional conferences. If you don't do what you are supposed to do, what alternatives are left open to me regarding your attendance at those meetings?

Pete: You mean you would prevent me from attending those meetings unless I take an hour for lunch like everybody else?

You: You are exactly right. You leave me no choice. Now don't you agree it's a problem?

Pete: Boy, it's one hell of a note that when you get a few personal problems around here, people threaten you with losing your job.

You: Pete, let me ask you a question? Do you think I have a choice as to whether I terminate your employment or not, if you keep doing this thing?

Pete: You certainly do.

You: The real answer is I do not. Either you correct the problem or I have to get somebody in the job who doesn't do that. Now with whatever personal problems you have, aren't they going to be worse if you don't have a job?

Pete: Well, of course they would be worse if I didn't have a job.

You: Well, do you agree then that it is a problem?

Pete: Well, if you are going to put it that way, it certainly is a problem.

You: Great. How are we going to solve it?

(You just finished Step 1 and are starting Step 2.)

Pete: Well, I won't do it anymore.

You: You won't do what anymore?

Pete: I won't take two and a half hours for lunch.

You: That's great. What will you do?

Pete: Well, I'll take an hour for lunch.

You: That's fine. What else will you do?

Pete: That's what you wanted, isn't it?

You: Yes, that will be beneficial to both of us. But, what was the other part of the problem we discussed?

Pete: Well, you said that people accused me of being drunk after lunch.

You: That's exactly right. What will you do about that?

Pete: Well, I'll just drink less on my lunch hour.

You: That's great. How much will you drink on your lunch hour?

Pete: Well, that's my private business. After all, you don't pay me for my lunch hour.

You: You are right. We don't pay you for lunch hour, but if what

you do on your lunch hour affects your work, then it's important to both of us. Tell me, before these personal problems
occurred, did you drink on your lunch hour?

Pete: Of course I did.

You: Approximately how much would you drink?

Pete: Well, I would have one martini for lunch.

You: And did anybody ever accuse you of acting drunk after having
one martini?

Pete: No.

You: Then how many drinks do you think it would be safe to have
on your lunch hour without people accusing you of being
drunk?

Pete: One martini.

You: That's great. When are you going to start?
(You have just finished Step 2, and you are now working on
Step 3.)

Pete: Right away.

You: When is that?

Pete: Next week.

You; When next week?

Pete: Next Monday.

You: That's great. Does that mean you will take one hour for lunch
next Monday?

Pete: Yes.

You: And does that mean you will drink no more than one martini
for lunch?

Pete: That's right.

You: Well, I'm glad you have agreed to solve this problem. Thank
you very much for your efforts. I will see you next Monday
right after lunch.
(You have just finished Step 3.)

The next two steps are FOLLOW-UP and RECOGNIZING ANY
ACHIEVEMENT. You certainly should be there next Monday at
the end of Pete's lunch hour to recognize that he does take less than
two and a half hours. And you should do that each day for the next
week. The following three weeks you should check every day to make
sure he is doing what he said he was going to do, but it will be necessary
to recognize him for it only twice a week.

In dealing with unsatisfactory performance allegedly caused by personal problems, it is important to determine whether or not you can survive with nonperformance until the personal problems go away. If you can, then don't deal with the problem. Just hold your breath until it goes away. If the performance must be corrected, you and the subordinate have no alternative but to correct it. Some people will accuse you of being heartless because you will not ignore performance problems caused by personal problems. But if you don't have the choice of accepting the unsatisfactory performance, it means that unsatisfactory performance is self-destructive behavior. Therefore, if you do whatever is necessary to make a subordinate stop his self-destructive behavior, your efforts are really in his interest. If, as a manager, you are unable to get him to stop his self-destructive behavior, then you are involved in self-destructive behavior.

If you use the coaching process as described, and in the order shown, you will be amazed at the results you will achieve. The coaching process works. But let me caution you that if you change the order of the steps of the coaching process or leave out a step, it will not work. So don't delude yourself into believing you are using the coaching process and expecting to get effective results, if you don't follow the steps completely. If you find yourself saying, "I use the coaching process, but on an informal basis," you are not using the coaching process; you are doing something else.

12
The Requirements For You To Be Successful In Eliminating Subordinates' Unsatisfactory Performance

YOU MUST ACCURATELY IDENTIFY WHAT BEHAVIOR CHANGE YOU DESIRE

When you manage performance results, it is easy enough to specify desired changes in expected results. There is no problem determining how much more or less of what it is you want within a specific time frame. As we mentioned earlier, though, the manager's job is not to manage results, but to manage those aspects of performance (behavior) that will cause the result. If the results you are obtaining from your subordinates now are not satisfactory, you have to define what the subordinate must *do differently* so the desired result will occur.

It is not enough, as a manager, merely to identify what is being done wrong. Although it is helpful to know what is happening, the most important benefit from knowing what is wrong is to use it as a basis to decide what it is the subordinate must do right. If you have done an effective coaching analysis, you will be able to know in advance of your face-to-face discussion what behavior change you desire. If you can't identify the behavior change you desire, that means any discussions you have with the subordinate are for the purpose of collecting more information to find out WHAT IS GOING ON.

THE SUBORDINATE'S BEHAVIOR MUST AFFECT THE RESULTS

It may seem obvious if obstacles beyond the subordinate's control are causing nonperformance, a change in the subordinate's behavior will not affect the results. What is not so obvious is that many times managers observe a lack of performance outcome at the same time they observe some aspect of the subordinate's behavior that is clearly unacceptable, undesirable, or downright aggravating. Unfortunately, managers do not always take the time to ascertain whether a change in that particular behavior will have any effect on the consequences. If a subordinate's behavior does not, or will not, affect the consequences, why are you talking to that subordinate?

THERE MUST BE MAXIMUM INVOLVEMENT OF THE SUBORDINATE IN THE FACE-TO-FACE DISCUSSION

I am not suggesting you have actual physical contact with the subordinate and win two out of three falls. By maximum involvement, I mean involvement of the subordinate's head. The only way for you to know whether you have that involvement of the subordinate's head is if you can make sounds come out of the subordinate's mouth. It is not enough to have a clear *yes* or *no* from the subordinate in response to the gems of wisdom you toss out as solutions. You must use thought transmission to make those wonderful solutions go from your head to the subordinate's head. You will know this has occurred when the sound of that gem of wisdom comes out of the subordinate's mouth instead of your own.

THERE MUST BE MAXIMUM COMMUNICATION AS SPECIFIC FEEDBACK TO SUBORDINATES ABOUT THEIR BEHAVIOR

As mentioned earlier, approximately 50 percent of the non-performance problems occurring in business can be related to feedback problems. That is, the performer is not aware of the results of his performance. Maximum feedback does not mean you have to yell loudly when telling someone he is doing something wrong. Having the subordinate keep his own score is more beneficial than when you keep score and report it to the subordinate.

If somebody says to you, "I didn't realize I was doing that," they are telling you they were lacking feedback relative to their behavior. Remember that the first discussion with a problem subordinate may be to supply feedback, i.e., for you to tell him what he is doing is not acceptable and that you require it be changed.

Also, feedback should concentrate on achievement scores rather than failure scores. Don't report people's failure level; report their achievement level. Those people failing by 10 percent are also 90 percent perfect. This feedback is equally important after the subordinate does agree to change. Subordinates often promise to do something different to change the outcome, and they truly believe they are doing something different when in actual fact they are not. A high frequency of feedback during the improvement process will support the improvement efforts. Your feedback as recognition of previously agreed-upon changes will reinforce the changing behavior.

YOU MUST IDENTIFY FOR YOUR SUBORDINATE THE NEED FOR THE CHANGE

Managers frequently complain about subordinates who either do not do those obvious things necessary for solving problems or who continue to do the same thing over and over again, although it doesn't work. The things a subordinate is doing wrong seem so obvious to the manager he or she can't understand why the subordinate doesn't make the obvious changes. Unfortunately these managers are interpreting their subordinates' actions in view of the alternatives they see available to the subordinate rather than the alternatives the subordinate sees available to the subordinate. Remember what we learned from George Kelly: people do not do illogical things on purpose. They may find out later that something is illogical either because it didn't work or because they discovered a better way to do it.

If the only reason for you to be there as a manager is to help your subordinates be as successful as possible, you must initiate action to help them improve. Remember that one of the answers to the question, "Why don't subordinates do what they are supposed to do?" was "They don't know why they should." If subordinates don't know the reason they should be changing, it is your responsibility to identify that need for change for them. It is not only important you communicate that they must change, it is equally important to communicate the reasons why they must change. In the steps of the face-to-face coaching discussion, Step 1, *getting agreement a problem exists*, accomplishes this by communicating to the subordinate the results of the thing done wrong and the consequences if it doesn't stop.

If the need for change appears to be blatantly obvious to your subordinates and they do not change, you should assume, "It may not be as obvious to them as I think."

SUBORDINATES MUST UNDERSTAND THAT THEY ARE RESPONSIBLE FOR THEIR OWN BEHAVIOR

One recently popular television comedian, Flip Wilson, was famous for one of his lines, "The devil made me do it." Implicit in this humorous line is that the individual was not responsible for his actions; the things that were done were beyond his control. Frequently subordinates blame others or obstacles in the environment as the reason for their own actions of unsatisfactory performance. Their assumption is they did what they did because others made them do it.

If you are trying to teach young children to walk, you will be faced with situations of unsatisfactory performance because the child does not yet have full control over his musculature. Therefore, his attempted body movement will result in the placement of his arms and legs in positions that are totally inappropriate and unintended. In the work environment, however, you are dealing with adults, and you are not asking them to perform in ways that are beyond their personal control.

The basic aspect of the employment process is that people are renting their behavior to you. A basic assumption is they are responsible for the behavior they are renting, otherwise how could they offer it for rent. Although a plea of temporary insanity may be appropriate in a court of law as a defendant's reason for commiting a heinous crime, it is not an alternative reason for nonperformance on the job.

If the performance problem you face is really occurring because the subordinate cannot control his own actions, the subordinate is too ill to be managed. If his illness prevents him from controlling his own actions, he certainly can't be responsible for his own behavior, and you certainly can't solve the problem. Your only alternative is to get him out of there and, perhaps, to encourage medical assistance.

SUBORDINATES MUST PERCEIVE THAT WHAT IS HAPPENING IS IN THEIR INTEREST

The only way to know what people perceive is to get them to write about it or verbalize it. The best way to do that is using the thought transmission techniques.

The purpose of the coaching process is to help you improve subordinates' performance; to help them stop their self-destructive behavior so you are not forced to administer consequences that are not in their self-interest. The coaching process defines solutions to problems, rather than creating a weighty record that will be tied around the subordinate's neck when you throw him overboard. The subordinate's perception of coaching will be based on your action to solve the problem. If you really believe the only reason for you to be there as a manager is to help them be as successful as possible, you will be *doing* helpful things, rather than just keeping score.

When people accuse you of hassling them or picking on them (if you really aren't), you should explain in detail the things you have learned in the earlier part of this book that relate to self-destructive behavior, management, and what managers get paid for. It is equally important to explain that their behavior dictates your behavior; that the more their behavior deviates from the appropriate behavior of their job, the fewer behavior alternatives you have to choose from. It is not enough for you to know you are trying to help them, and it is not enough for you to say, "I am trying to help you." It is up to you to say and do all those things that will transmit the thought to their minds: "Ah, the boss is trying to help me stop my self-destructive behavior."

YOU MUST BE COMMITTED TO THE SAME THINGS YOU WANT SUBORDINATES TO DO

In a division of one large company, an executive who came to work late, left early, took long lunch hours, cheated on expenses and over-drank his lunches, complained continuously about his subordinates doing the same things. If you do not come to work on time each day, not only is it difficult for you to know which of your subordinates come to work on time, but your subordinates will have difficulty differentiating between what is important and what you say is important. If honesty is a practice you want subordinates to follow, then honest is what you must be. If you make speeches to your subordinates about loyalty and commitment to the corporation, but your own behavior demonstrates lack of loyalty and lack of commitment, it will be an inconsistency that prevents you from managing them successfully. You will not be able to get them to follow rules if you do not follow them yourself. For example, if you want them to have minorities on their staff but you have none on your staff, you have a credibility gap. If you are not committed to the same things you want your subordinates to do, you will not be successful in getting them to do it. The converse is not true, however; you will not get subordinates to do what you want them to do merely by being committed to doing it yourself. Being a good example alone is not enough for you to change subordinates' behavior. In addition to being a good example, you must do those other management things discussed in this book.

YOU MUST ACKNOWLEDGE AND PRAISE SUBORDINATES' ACHIEVEMENTS

The last step in the face-to-face coaching process is *recognize any achievement*. Recognition is the first important reason for follow-up. Behavior modification, the scientific approach to managing human behavior, emphasizes the importance of your praise and recognition as a positive consequence to influence your subordinate's actions. It is not enough for you to observe and record change when it occurs, you must respond to it by saying and doing things to the subordinate as recognition of their improvements. Remember that achievement is not only winning, it is also losing by less than you ever did before.

WHAT YOU CAN DO TO GUARANTEE FAILURE IN CHANGING YOUR SUBORDINATES' BEHAVIOR

1. DON'T GET THE SUBORDINATE INVOLVED, JUST TALK *AT* HIM OR HER.

2. DON'T GIVE SPECIFIC FEEDBACK; TALK IN GENERALITIES.

3. CONCENTRATE ON ATTITUDE, RATHER THAN BEHAVIOR.

4. ASSUME THE SUBORDINATE UNDERSTANDS THAT A PROBLEM EXISTS.

5. ASSUME THE SUBORDINATE KNOWS WHAT HAS TO BE DONE TO SOLVE THE PROBLEM.

6. DON'T FOLLOW UP TO INSURE THAT THE AGREED-UPON ACTION HAS BEEN TAKEN BY THE SUBORDINATE.

7. DON'T ACKNOWLEDGE OR PRAISE THE SUBORDINATE WHEN HE OR SHE CORRECTS THE PROBLEM.

13
Critical Questions
And Problems

DOESN'T THE COACHING DISCUSSION CREATE TEN-
SION AND STRESS FOR THE SUBORDINATE?
Yes, but the tension and stress are considerably less than what occurs
when you tell the subordinate he or she is fired because of self-
destructive behavior.

ISN'T ALL OF THIS MANIPULATION?
Sure it is. But so is everything else you do that has the effect of getting
other people to do what you want them to do, such as promising raises,
terminations, and promotions.

BUT ISN'T IT LESS HUMANISTIC TO DEAL ONLY WITH
PEOPLE'S BEHAVIOR?
A popular management belief is that it is more humanistic to deal with
people's motives and value systems, assuming that if you change them,
you will get a change in behavior. This is a shockingly contradictory
concept. No employer has the right, or the ability, to mess around with
people's motives and value systems. It is, in fact, more humanistic to
deal with the behaviors you rent without requiring people to change.

ARE YOU TELLING ME THAT I SHOULD TALK TO PEOPLE
ONLY ABOUT THEIR WORK BEHAVIOR AND HAVE NO
OTHER DISCUSSIONS WITH THEM?
Of course not. This book deals only with those face-to-face discussions
relative to increasing productivity and helping subordinates eliminate

202

their self-destructive behavior. You should maintain your other work relationships. For example, if subordinates normally seek your advice about personal problems, continue to advise them, as long as your action is not supporting unsatisfactory performance.

HOW LONG DOES IT TAKE BEFORE YOU GET GOOD AT THIS?

It depends on how closely you follow the steps, and how frequently you do the things in this book. You will get better at it each time you do it. The greater the frequency, the faster you will improve.

IS THERE SOME SECRET OR RULE YOU CAN GIVE ME TO HELP ME BE AS SUCCESSFUL AS POSSIBLE USING COACHING?

There is a rule, though it is no secret. It applies to everything else in life.

1) Prepare: decide ahead of time what has to be done and what you are going to do.
2) When using it, follow a specific plan of action; don't play it by ear.
3) Give yourself feedback; compare your actions and the outcome to what you have planned.
4) Decide what you will do different next time to more closely approximate your plan.

WHAT HAPPENS IF I DO EVERYTHING YOU SAY, BUT THEY STILL DON'T CHANGE?

Transfer or terminate them, or learn to live with the problem.

WHAT HAPPENS IF I USE THE COACHING PROCESS, BUT NOT SO FORMALLY?

It won't work.

WHAT HAPPENS IF MY SUBORDINATE CRIES DURING THE COACHING DISCUSSION?

Keep quiet and wait for him or her to stop.

WHAT HAPPENS IF MY SUBORDINATE ALSO READS THIS BOOK?

If your subordinate is a supervisor of others, he or she will probably get better at it. And if you have to coach them they will have a better understanding of what you are trying to do.

BUT IF MY SUBORDINATE KNOWS WHAT I AM TRYING TO DO, WILL IT WORK?

Of course it will. Coaching is not trickery. If you interview somebody for a job and he knows you are interviewing him, does that prevent you from doing it? Of course it doesn't. Your questioning techniques (thought transmission) during coaching direct the subordinate's concentration to giving real answers to real questions.

WHAT DO I DO WHEN A SUBORDINATE REQUESTS THAT A UNION REPRESENTATIVE BE PRESENT DURING THE COACHING DISCUSSION?

If the union contract includes this provision, do it. But direct your conversation to the subordinate, not to the representative. Most union representatives like the coaching process because it deals with specifics.

HOW IS COACHING AFFECTED BY MY UNION CONTRACT REQUIREMENT TO GIVE WARNINGS AND REPRIMANDS?

It is not affected at all. Go ahead and hold your feedback discussions or coaching discussions, and give out the formal paperwork at the end of each.

IF I COMPLIMENT PEOPLE FOR FAILING BY LESS, EVEN THOUGH THEY ARE STILL FAILING, WON'T THEY STOP TRYING?

That depends on what you tell them. If someone improves performance from 80 percent effectiveness to 90 percent effectiveness and you tell him he is terrific, he may assume that 90 percent is all that is needed to be effective. Your comments of recognition must be specific about the improvement, and include a statement about the expected end result. For example, "Your work today is the best I have ever seen it. You have made a big improvement by going from 80 percent to 90 percent. If you keep that up, pretty soon you will be reaching our departmental standard of 98 percent. Keep up the good work."

WHAT HAPPENS IF I CAN'T GET AGREEMENT, BUT I DON'T
WANT TO FIRE THEM?

1) Look for additional consequences.
2) Re-analyze why you think it's important.
3) If they ever do what you want, stop coaching them, give them
   positive reinforcement, and see if the frequency increases.
4) Learn to live with it.

ISN'T IT UNREASONABLE TO EXPECT MANAGERS TO
TAKE FULL RESPONSIBILITY FOR THE SUCCESS OR
FAILURE OF THEIR SUBORDINATES?
Of course not. A manager gets paid to maximize the organization's
return on investment in their resources. Each manager's success is
based on the ability to do that. If a manager doesn't accept responsibility for that success or failure, the responsibility passes to the resource itself. For a manager to expect the resource to be responsible
for its own success or failure is self-destructive behavior (by the
manager).

IT SEEMS AS THOUGH COACHING WOULD WORK FOR A
LOT OF EMPLOYEES, BUT I DON'T THINK IT WOULD BE
EFFECTIVE WITH PROFESSIONALS AT THE Ph.D. LEVEL.
That's not a question, that's a statement. It is just as erroneous to
assume that all Ph.D.s are self-motivated, all M.D.s are competent, all
government officials are honest, and all college professors are logical.
Unfortunately, the more education you have, the more money you are
paid, the higher the level of position you fill in the organization, the
less you will be managed, and, therefore, the less you will be helped by
your boss to succeed. Coaching does work at all levels, and should be
used at all levels as is necessary.

ARE YOU TELLING ME THAT EVERYBODY I HIRE RE-
GARDLESS OF LEVEL OF EDUCATION, EXPERIENCE, AND
POSITION IN THE ORGANIZATION IS GOING TO FAIL?
Of course not. But I am telling you that everybody you hire in the
organization regardless of level of education, salary, and position in
the organization must be managed to be as successful as possible.

HOW LONG WILL I HAVE TO DO COACHING BEFORE IT BECOMES NATURAL FOR ME?
If by *natural* you mean, when will you be able to do it without thinking about it, the answer is never. A good rule to remember is this, *Whenever you are doing what you are doing without thinking about it, worry about it, because you are probably not doing it as well as you could.*

CAN I USE COACHING ON MY BOSS?
Coaching is effective only on those people who answer directly to you. Some of the techniques, however, such as thought transmission, positive reinforcement, exploration of alternatives, and getting agreement that a problem exists, are useful in dealing with peers and superiors.

COACHING LOOKS AS IF IT WILL TAKE QUITE A BIT OF TIME; HOW DO I FIND TIME TO DO THAT AS WELL AS EVERYTHING ELSE?
The initial coaching discussions do not take a lot more time than the Y, S, and T approach. If you use coaching, however, you will solve more problems in the long run, and you will talk about the same problem less frequently. If you are saying you cannot take two hours now to solve a problem, perhaps the problem is unimportant and you should forget it.

SOME OF THOSE QUESTIONS AND ANSWERS IN THE COACHING DISCUSSIONS SEEM RATHER CHILDISH. WON'T THE HIGH-LEVEL, SOPHISTICATED PEOPLE WHO ANSWER TO ME COME UP WITH THE SAME OBSERVATION?
During my six years of teaching this process, never has a manager or subordinate reported the occurrence of this kind of observation during coaching. It is unlikely because, in the process of your coaching them, you will be asking for real answers to real questions. Nevertheless, if you feel better using words with more syllables or speaking in Latin, please feel free to do so, as long as you both understand what you both are talking about.

WHAT DO I DO WHEN I AM COMPLIMENTING SOMEONE
TO REINFORCE WHAT HE IS DOING AND HE SAYS ACCUS-
INGLY, "HA! YOU ARE GIVING ME POSITIVE REINFORCE-
MENT."

You should say, "Yes, you are right. It is easy to do that with you because of this good thing (specify it) you are doing."

Selected Bibliography

Argyris, Chris. *Integrating the Individual and the Organization.* New York: John Wiley & Sons, 1964.

Batten, J. D. *Beyond Management by Objectives.* New York: American Management Assn., 1966.

Bijou, Sidney and Ribes-Inesta, Emilio. *Behavior Modification: Issues and Extensions.* New York: Academic Press, 1972.

Blake, Robert and Mouton, Jane. *The Managerial Grid.* Houston: Gulf Publishing, 1964.

Campbell, John P.; Dunnette, M. D.; Lawler, E. E.; and Weick, K. E. *Managerial Behavior, Performance, and Effectiveness.* New York: McGraw-Hill, 1970.

Deibert, Alvin and Harman, Alice J. *New Tools for Changing Behavior.* Champaign, IL: Research Press, 1973.

Dickson, William and Roethlisberger, Fritz. *Counseling in an Organization.* Cambridge: Harvard University Press, 1966.

Downing, Lester N. *Counseling Theories and Techniques: Summarized and Critiqued.* Chicago: Nelson-Hall, 1975.

Drucker, Peter F. *Management: Tasks, Practices, Responsibilities.* New York: Harper & Row, 1974.

Fournies, Ferdinand F. *Management Performance Appraisal—A National Study.* Bridgewater, NJ: F. Fournies & Associates, 1973.

_____. *Salesman Performance Appraisal—A National Study.* Bridgewater, NJ: F. Fournies & Associates, 1975.

Hackney, Harold and Nye, Sherilyn. *Counseling Strategies and Objectives.* Englewood Cliffs, NJ: Prentice-Hall, 1973.

Hamerlynch, Leo A.; Handy, Lee C.; and Mash, Eric J. *Behavior Change— Methodology, Concepts & Practice.* Champaign, IL: Research Press, 1973.

Herzberg, Frederick; Mausner, W.; and Snyderman, R. *The Motivation to Work.* New York: John Wiley & Sons, 1959.

Herzberg, Frederick. *Work and the Nature of Man.* Cleveland: World Publishing, 1966.

Hilgard, Ernest R. *Theories of Learning.* Englewood Cliffs, NJ: Appleton-Century-Crofts, 1956.

Hills, William G.; Van Rest, Andre; Kearney, Richard; and Smith, Stephen. *Administration and Management.* Norman, OK: University of Oklahoma Press, 1975.

Kazdin, Alan E. *Behavior Modification in Applied Settings.* Homewood, IL: The Dorsey Press, 1975.

Kellogg, Marion. *Closing the Performance Gap.* New York: American Management Assn., 1967.

Koontz, Harold and O'Donnell, Cyril. *Principles of Management—An Analysis of Managerial Functions.* 2nd ed. New York: McGraw-Hill, 1959.

Leitenberg, Harold, ed. *Handbook of Behavior Modification and Behavior Therapy.* Englewood Cliffs, NJ: Prentice-Hall, 1976.

Lindzey, Gardner. *Assessment of Human Motives.* New York: Holt, Rinehart & Winston, 1958.

Lippitt, Ronald; Watson, Jeanne; and Westley, Bruce. *The Dynamics of Planned Change.* New York: Harcourt Brace Jovanovich, 1958.

McGregor, Douglas. *The Human Side of Enterprise.* New York: McGraw-Hill, 1960.

Maher, Brendan. *Clinical Psychology & Personality: The Selected Papers of George Kelly.* New York: John Wiley & Sons, 1969.

Malott, Richard. *Contingency Management in Education and Other Equally Exciting Places.* Kalamazoo: Behaviordelia, 1972.

Mann, John. *Changing Human Behavior.* New York: Charles Scribner's Sons, 1965.

Maslow, Abraham H. *Motivation and Personality.* New York: Harper & Row, 1954.

National Society for the Study of Education. *Theories of Learning and Instruction.* Chicago: University of Chicago, 1964.

Neuringer, Charles and Michael, Jack L. *Behavior Modification in Clinical Psychology.* Englewood Cliffs, NJ: Appleton-Century-Crofts, 1970.

O'Leary, K. Daniel and Wilson, G. Terence. *Behavior Therapy: Application and Outcome.* Englewood Cliffs, NJ: Prentice-Hall, 1975.

Osipow, Samuel H. and Walsh, W. Bruce. *Behavior Change in Counseling: Readings and Cases.* Englewood Cliffs, NJ: Prentice-Hall, 1970.

_____. *Strategies in Counseling for Behavior Change.* Englewood Cliffs, NJ: Prentice-Hall, 1970.

Passons, William R. *Gestalt Approaches in Counseling.* New York: Holt, Rinehart & Winston, 1975.

Rosenthal, Robert. *Pygmalion in the Classroom.* New York: Holt, Rinehart & Winston, 1968.

Rowland, Virgil. *Evaluating and Improving Managerial Performance.* New York: McGraw-Hill, 1970.

Schwitzgebel, Ralph K. and Kolb, David A. *Changing Human Behavior: Principles of Planned Intervention.* New York: McGraw-Hill, 1974.

Skinner, B. F. *About Behaviorism.* New York: Alfred A. Knopf, 1974.

Sundel, Martin and Sundel, Sandra. *Behavior Modification in the Human Services: A Systematic Introduction to Concepts and Applications.* New York: John Wiley & Sons, 1975.

Travers, Robert. *Essentials of Learning.* New York: Macmillan, 1967.

U.S. Congress. Senate. Committee on the Judiciary. *Individual Rights and the Federal Role in Behavior Modification.* 93rd Cong., 2nd sess., November, 1974.

U.S. Department of Defense. Naval Training Command. *Human Behavior and Leadership.* Washington, DC: Government Printing Office, 1973.

Wolpe, Joseph. The Practice of Behavior Therapy. 2nd ed. New York: Pergamon, 1974.

Index